To

Roy:

Happy Birthday.

Kitty & Arthur.

KENT'S HISTORIC BUILDINGS

KENT'S
Historic Buildings

WILLIAM WEBB

Photographs by May Guest

ROBERT HALE LIMITED

© *William Webb 1977*
First published in Great Britain 1977

ISBN 0 7091 6147 6

Robert Hale Limited
Clerkenwell House
Clerkenwell Green
London EC1R 0HT

Photoset and bound
by Weatherby Woolnough, Wellingborough
Printed in Great Britain by
Lowe & Brydone Ltd, Thetford

Contents

Illustrations

MAP

This map is based, with permission, on the Ordnance Survey

Acknowledgements

I am indebted to Miss E. Plincke and Mr G. Stevens of Bromley Reference Library for help in consulting old records and to the staff of South Norwood (Croydon) Library for tracing and obtaining out-of-print volumes. The Department of the Environment and the National Trust provided details of the properties in their care. The owners of properties in private hands kindly supplied me with information and allowed access at times when their property was not generally open to the public.

I was given much help by librarians of Kent newspapers in consulting their files.

Finally I am indebted to May Guest who went to a great deal of trouble to obtain the photographs to illustrate this book.

For all Men of Kent and Kentishmen and Fair Maids of Kent

Introduction

STEP INTO KENT and you step into history. Within the confines of the county are the hill forts of the Ancient Britons, Roman camps and villas, Norman castles, monasteries, palaces and stately homes.

This is to be expected in a county which is the nearest to the Continent and has been the first to experience or to be threatened with invasion. Julius Caesar and his Roman legions landed on the shingle at Walmer in 55 B.C. and again in 54 B.C. The Romans came again in A.D. 43, this time to stay for nearly 400 years. The Saxon chiefs Hengist and Horsa invaded through the Isle of Thanet and set up the Kingdom of Kent, the earliest kingdom in England. William the Conqueror, although landing in Sussex, marched into Kent and led his army via Dover and Canterbury on to London.

French forces raided Kent ports during the Hundred Years War. There was very real danger from the Spanish Armada and from Napoleon's Grande Armée. In the Second World War, Hitler's invasion plan envisaged landings on the Kent coast between Folkestone and Dungeness.

Much earlier, in 596, there had been a different type of invasion when St Augustine and his monks landed at Ebbsfleet and brought Christianity to the heathen Anglo-Saxon land.

Saxon kings of Kent are buried at Canterbury and two kings of England, with their queens, are also buried in the county.

Clerics, soldiers, sailors, statesmen and famous men in the history of the nation have come from Kent or made it their home. Their histories are still there in the castles, abbeys, cathedrals and great houses which they left behind.

Kent, therefore, can show the whole range of history and it is the aim of this book to provide an introduction to these fascinating places which give both knowledge and enjoyment. More than seventy are described, but this does not exhaust the list. Most of them are open to the public at various times. The few which are not are all visible from the road.

1

North-West Kent

ALTHOUGH THIS AREA is now part of the Greater London Council it is historically a part of Kent. The county society, the Association of Men of Kent and Kentishmen, has branches and many members living in what is officially 'South-East London' but which they still call 'North-West Kent'. Their allegiance is to Maidstone and Canterbury although their rate money goes to County Hall, Lambeth.

This is an area with strong royal connections. Kings and queens have been born, married and have died here and an emperor spent his last days in exile on Kentish soil.

Greenwich is a familiar word all over the world. The Greenwich meridian and Greenwich time have made this pleasant riverside area a household word and, although the Royal Observatory has now moved to Herstmonceux Castle in Sussex, the name is still retained.

But Greenwich was famous, long before the Observatory was founded, as a vast royal palace, the favourite home of many kings and queens. Duke Humphrey of Gloucester, brother of Henry V, bought 17 acres of land on the banks of the Thames in 1426 and built himself a rambling palace. On the hill above he erected a hunting tower, later the site of the Royal Observatory. He encircled the whole place with a 200-acre park and named it Bella Court.

On his death it passed to Margaret of Anjou, queen of Henry VI, who made extensive alterations and renamed it Placentia. Her royal monogram was on new tiles which were laid. On the stone pillars were sculpted marguerite daisies, the emblem of her name. Glass, a rare luxury in those days, was placed in the windows. She had two extra courts added along the riverside and a pier built out into the river so that she could embark or disembark from her barge whatever the state of the tide.

On the defeat of the Lancastrians at Tewkesbury the palace of Placentia was seized by the new king, Edward IV. His eldest daughter, Elizabeth of York (later the queen of Henry VII), was born and spent her childhood here.

When the Yorkists were defeated at Bosworth, Henry VII took over the palace and strengthened it with brick-built battlements along the riverside. His son, the future Henry VIII, was born in the palace and baptized in the royal chapel. It was to be his favourite residence and it was at Greenwich that he married the first of his six wives, Katherine of Aragon. He described it as "a pleasant, perfect and princely palace". This was the period of Greenwich's greatness. Jousts and tournaments were staged in the park in which Henry participated "with a spere of 8 fote long". He organized hunting and hawking in the park and most of the great feast days were spent at Greenwich. The first masked ball to be held in England was staged in the great hall.

Henry's daughters, Mary and Elizabeth, were both born at Placentia and the palace was to remain a firm favourite with Elizabeth after she came to the throne, in spite of the fact that the death warrant of her mother, Anne Boleyn, was signed there.

It was at Greenwich that the famous episode concerning Sir Walter Raleigh took place. He was waiting at the gate hoping for an audience when the queen and her ladies returned from a walk in the park. Seeing her hesitate when coming to a muddy patch, he stepped forward and threw his cloak on the ground so that she could cross. Another Raleigh episode is said to be an inscription which he cut with a diamond on one of the glass windows, "Feign would I climb, but that I fear to fall". The queen saw it and added "If thy heart fail thee, climb not at all."

James I gave the palace and park to his queen, Anne of Denmark, and also commissioned Inigo Jones to build her a special house, to be known as 'The Queen's House', in the park. This was on the site of Raleigh's encounter and spanned the public road through the park. The house was built over and on both sides of the road but it had not been finished when Anne of Denmark died in 1619. Work stopped, but when Charles I came to the throne he ordered it to be finished for his queen Henrietta Maria. It was completed in a Palladian style with a magnificent horseshoe staircase reminiscent of the famous one at Fontainebleau. Paintings by Rubens, Titian and Van Dyck, fine period furniture and glass were brought in and the queen was delighted with it. A tablet over a window inscribed "Henrica Maria Regina 1635" can still be seen.

Unfortunately for her, she did not enjoy her new property for many years. The Civil War broke out, the king was beheaded, and she and her children fled to France. The old palace of Placentia was used as a prison and then as a factory. Buildings and paintings were sold but the Queen's House escaped without serious damage and was used for the lying-in-state of Admiral Robert Blake.

At the Restoration, Charles II inspected Placentia and decided it would cost too much to restore and so he ordered it to be demolished. Henrietta Maria returned to the Queen's House. The king then decided he would build a King's House to restore the splendours of Greenwich but he ran out of money before it could be completed.

The royal connection with Greenwich was at an end, for the new monarchs, William and Mary, preferred Hampton Court, but it was now to enter upon a new and equally distinguished chapter of its history. The first step had already been taken for Charles II had ordered the building of the first Royal Observatory on the site of Duke Humphrey's hunting lodge. Queen Mary decided that she would found a hospital on the site of the old palace of Placentia for distressed seamen to complement the hospital for soldiers at Chelsea. Wren was commissioned to carry out this work and, assisted by Hawksmoor and Vanbrugh, erected the magnificent buildings which are still so much admired on the banks of the Thames. There is a gap in the middle, left there deliberately so that the view of the Thames from the Queen's House should not be lost.

The first pensioners were housed in the buildings in 1705. All were seamen or marines who had served in the Royal Navy and had wounds or sickness due to their service. They were provided with food, beer, tobacco, a suit of blue clothes and a cocked hat.

Dr Samuel Johnson said that the building was too magnificent for charity and the Czar, Peter the Great, although very impressed, said it was more suited to royalty than to "worn-out-seamen". The pensioners themselves do not seem to have been too happy in their magnificent surroundings for many chose to accept pensions and live outside. Eventually it was decided in 1865 to close it as a hospital and shortly afterwards it became the Royal Naval College.

This stately and imposing group of buildings, described as "the nearest equivalent to a palace of Louis XIV", is still used by the Royal Navy for specialist training courses. Parts of it, including the famous Painted Hall in King William's block, are open to the public. This has the huge painted ceiling by Sir James Thornhill which took him nineteen years to complete. He was paid £3 a foot for the ceiling and £1 a foot for the walls. It was in this hall that Nelson lay in state before his journey up the river in a barge to be buried in St Paul's Cathedral.

The centre-piece of the ceiling shows William and Mary handing the cup of liberty to Europe where Louis XIV is being trampled under by democracy. The walls are dedicated to the greatness of William and of George I and, among Greek gods and goddesses, can be seen William landing at Brixham and being greeted by Britannia with her friends 'Reason of State' and 'Patriotism'. Thornhill portrays himself standing on the steps of St Paul's.

The Queen's House had become a naval school and to accommodate the pupils two wings were built. These are connected to the main building by two open colonnades 180 feet long. Built in 1807 to commemorate the victory at Trafalgar, they were used as a playground by the boys in wet weather. The officers lived in the Queen's House.

The Navy vacated the premises in 1933 and the buildings became the National Maritime Museum. The Queen's House, with its black and white seventeenth-century floor and Inigo Jones Tulip Staircase, contains priceless furniture and paintings, mainly of ships, battles and storms. The museum presents the complete maritime history of the nation from the time of the Tudor monarchs to the present day. The uniform worn by Nelson at the Battle of Trafalgar is on display together with his blue and white striped stockings (darned by Lady Hamilton) and a chair from H.M.S. *Victory*.

State barges decorated with the arms of their owners, models of every type of ship (including modern warships), and figureheads and paintings present a fascinating story of a maritime nation. Probably the oldest exhibit is the Chatham Chest, an iron-bound box which was used to contain the money of a fund begun after the defeat of the Spanish Armada by Drake and Hawkins. From a seaman's wages a sum of 6*d*. (2½p) a month was put into the chest for a pension in his old age.

On the hill overlooking the National Maritime Museum is the old Royal Greenwich Observatory. It was founded for the improvement of navigation rather than the advancement of pure astronomy, for mariners of the seventeenth century had great difficulty in determining their position with the instruments then in use. In 1674 a Frenchman, St Pierre, suggested to Charles II that the moon's progress in the sky against the background of fixed stars would serve as a clock. The king appointed John Flamsteed to investigate and when he was told that neither the moon's progress nor the exact position of the stars was known accurately enough, he ordered this to be examined thoroughly. Flamsteed was appointed "our astronomical observer" and was charged with determining "the motions of the heavens as the fixed places of the stars to obtain longitude of places to perfect the art of navigation". Flamsteed was thus the first of a long line of Astronomers Royal although the title did not come into use until much later.

Wren designed the "small observatory within our park at Greenwich" at a cost of not more than £500 and it was he who chose the site on the meridian. Flamsteed laid the foundation stone and moved into the building in 1676. He was given no money to buy instruments and so he raised funds by taking in pupils for mathematics and astronomy. He therefore regarded his astronomical discoveries and results as his own private property.

Flamsteed was at the Observatory for thirty-four years and was succeeded by Edmund Halley, known for the discovery of the comet which bears his name. The problem of fixing longitude at sea was now so pressing that Parliament offered rewards of up to £20,000 for a successful method. Halley decided that more study was needed of the moon's progress across the sky. In the next eighteen years he observed more than 1,500 meridian transits of the moon. His observations, in four bound volumes, can be seen in the Observatory today.

It was Neville Maskelyne who produced the *Nautical Almanac* which provides the astronomical information required by navigators. He was succeeded by John Pond who is remembered for the installation of the first public time-signal in this country. At 1 p.m. every day a time-ball drops down on its mast above the Observatory.

In later years more staff were employed and more sophisticated equipment used. The early Astronomers Royal had mainly worked alone and Pond had only one assistant. Today more than 240 are engaged at the Observatory at Herstmonceux.

Scientific observations continued at Greenwich through the two world wars but under increasing difficulties. Electrification of the railways and the building of power stations made it impossible for work to continue there. Sometimes the staff could not determine whether a new line on the record was a disturbance on the surface of the sun or the passing of an electric train on the track a mile away. It was therefore essential to move to a quieter and less congested area, particularly as a flying bomb damaged the buildings in 1944.

In 1946 Herstmonceux Castle in Sussex was purchased for the sum of £76,000. The Observatory moved in there but "because of the long association of the Royal Observatory with Greenwich since the year 1675, the adoption by international agreement of the Greenwich meridian as the zero of longitude, and the world-wide use of a system of time zones based on the meridian" it would be known as "The Royal Greenwich Observatory, Herstmonceux".

The old Observatory, now part of the National Maritime Museum, contains many of the instruments used by the early astronomers. The scientists have gone but the name lives on.

Only three miles away from Greenwich but now buried in

suburbia is another royal palace. Little now remains of Eltham Palace except for its Great Hall but this is magnificent and well worth a visit.

Eltham is mentioned in the Domesday Book as being in the possession of Odo, Bishop of Bayeux, and half-brother of William the Conqueror. It was let to Haimo, the sheriff of the county, and eventually came into the possession of the de Vesci family. Henry III spent the Christmas of 1270 at Eltham and Edward I was often there as a guest of the de Vescis. It was sold in 1295 to Anthony Bek, Bishop of Durham, a wealthy cleric, who spent great sums of money in rebuilding the palace. In 1305 he made it over as a gift to Edward Prince of Wales, son of Edward I, and Eltham's royal connection began.

It became the favourite residence of the ill-fated Edward II and his queen Isabella. It was here that a son, John of Eltham, was born but he did not survive his father. Another son, the future Edward III, spent much of his childhood at Eltham. When he succeeded to the throne on the murder of his father, he commenced large-scale rebuilding and alterations at a cost of £2,000. These included a whole range of royal apartments, a new drawbridge, an oratory and domestic buildings. He extended and remodelled the park and planted a vineyard. Being in the country but reasonably close to London, Eltham was a favourite royal residence. A village grew up around it to accommodate the royal servants.

The king obviously took a keen interest in the operation and punished any slipshod work. Some masons who had built a wall were found to have skimped the work so that it was not of sufficient thickness. They were imprisoned and only released when they promised to rebuild the wall to the requisite thickness at their own expense.

Three kings, David of Scotland, Waldemar of Denmark and the captive King John of France, were entertained by Edward III in Eltham Palace.

Richard II put in a new bridge of "stone called ashlar" and built the outer court. Henry IV was married at Eltham by proxy to Joan of Navarre in 1402 and spent his Christmas at Eltham Palace on five occasions. Henry VI, often described as more monk than king, spent large sums rebuilding the chapel. Edward IV was responsible for the construction of the Great Hall with its hammer-beam roof which survives to this day.

With the coming of the Tudors, Eltham was increasingly favoured as a royal residence. Henry VII spent money on more buildings and Henry VIII spent many of his early years here. He had a private garden to which he would withdraw over a drawbridge and it was here that he indulged his passion for staging pageants. When the plague was raging in London in 1526 he passed many months at Eltham to be safe from it. He ordered the demolition of the old chapel of Henry VI and the erection of a new one "of timber work on a foundation of stone".

Eltham was, however, nearing the end of its glory. Henry preferred Greenwich where there was a better park. His son and daughters paid only brief visits and James I used the palace only as a hunting lodge. Charles I came only once in 1629.

After the Civil War the buildings were badly in need of repair. They were sold to Colonel Nathaniel Rich for £2,754. He started to demolish the place until only the Great Hall was left and this was used as a barn. It was not until modern times that serious restoration was undertaken and it is therefore highly pleasing and surprising that such a fine building as the Great Hall can still be seen in all its glory.

A moat surrounds the buildings and is crossed by a medieval bridge, probably that built in the reign of Richard II. The Great Hall, open to the public on certain days, is 100 feet long, 36 feet wide, and has a height of 55 feet. It is brick-built and its particular glory is the hammer-beam roof. Excavation is still proceeding to uncover the foundations of the vast range of buildings which were once part of the royal palace of Eltham.

Although its great days have long since passed, Eltham may still be remembered as the place where the senior order of chivalry, the Order of the Garter, was founded. It was at a ball at Eltham Palace in 1348 that Joan, Countess of Salisbury, known as the Fair Maid of Kent, had the misfortune to lose her garter. It was picked up by Edward III who said "Honi soit qui mal y pense" to the laughing courtiers. He then founded the order, which is limited to twenty-four Knights Companion.

In the woods off the road at Belvedere are the scanty remains of the great abbey of Lesnes. It had a chequered career and did not even last until the Reformation.

Lesnes was a monastery of the Austin Canons and was founded by Richard de Lucy, Justiciary of England, in honour of St Thomas Becket. He laid its foundation stone on 11 June 1178. It was a large establishment for the church was 132 feet in length with numerous chapels leading off it.

Although well endowed and founded in the heyday of monastic life, Lesnes seemed always to be in difficulties. Visitations by archbishops brought long lists of complaints and in later years it is clear that the abbot and his monks had lost their zest for monastic life and were out to enjoy themselves.

In 1283 Archbishop Peckham found that the monks were having secret meals in their cells, eating flesh on fast days, and not using the refectory. It was then discovered that nuns were allowed to stay the night in the monastery in spite of a rule that no women were to set foot inside the building.

By 1327 the abbot had so neglected necessary repairs to the fabric that decay had set in. Money for repairs had been spent on other things. The abbot, John of Hodesdon, was convicted of immorality in 1336, was punished and promised to mend his ways. Only four years later he was found guilty of gross mismanagement of the affairs of the abbey and was demoted. Shortly afterwards he and another two monks deserted from the abbey and warrants were issued for their arrest.

Lesnes continued in debt throughout the fifteenth century and the buildings were badly in need of repair. By 1524 it was obvious that the abbey was dying and Cardinal Wolsey issued orders for its suppression. Over the years its stones were carted away and it lay forlorn and neglected. Careful excavation has now revealed the foundation of Lesnes and this gives a fine impression of the size and detail of the buildings.

Within sight and sound of the lorries and cars rushing along the motorway is to be found one of the historic treasures of this part of the county, Hall Place at Bexley. This fine old building dates back to Tudor times and has fortunately been spared the horrors of restoration.

Hall Place is built of patterned stone and flint, giving a facing of black and white. Later additions are in red brick and these date from 1653 for this year is inscribed over the kitchen. The gardens and grounds alone make a visit worth while for they exhibit topiary work, herb gardens, sunken gardens and a heath running down to the River Cray. All this is a great credit to the local authority which now owns and occupies Hall Place.

The site was occupied by a Robert At-Hall in 1241 but the present building dates from 1537 when it was owned by Sir John Champneys, a former Lord Mayor of London. He completely rebuilt the house, using stone from the suppressed monasteries. It remained in his family until 1649 when it went to Robert Austen, a merchant from Tenterden. He would appear to have been a royalist for he was given a baronetcy and made Sheriff of Kent upon the restoration of Charles II.

Hall Place eventually came into the possession of Sir Francis Dashwood, notorious for his activities in the Hell-Fire Club and with the disreputable 'monks' of Medmenham Abbey.

The Dashwoods, however, found it too expensive to maintain and Hall Place became a school in 1799 and this was its role for the next seventy years. It was designed for "the sons of gentlemen" and over eighty were in residence. Subjects taught ranged from mathematics to dancing and the working day was from 6.30 a.m. to 6.30 p.m.

When the school was closed in 1870 Hall Place was let to a succession of tenants. The last of these, the Countess of Limerick arrived in 1917 and under her Hall Place revived all its former glories. Lavish receptions were held, attended by Prince Albert (later George VI) and Queen Marie of Rumania and in 1932 4,000 people took part in a pageant which attracted 50,000 spectators.

Lady Limerick died in 1943 and Hall Place was purchased by Bexley Council for £25,000.

There is a legend that it was at Hall Place that Edward, the Black Prince, courted Joan the Fair Maid of Kent whom he married and who was the mother of Richard II. No evidence has been produced for this but his ghost, clad in his

black armour, is said to haunt the house. He may possibly
have visited the house on his way to the French wars but it
is doubtful if he stayed there.

Watching a game of cricket at Chislehurst was a stout,
bearded old gentleman. He always took a great interest in
the matches and was known to reward a successful player
with a golden guinea. Those who did not know him would
think that he was a typical country gentleman who had
perhaps been an enthusiastic player in his youth. His interest
in so typical an English game as cricket demonstrated that
he valued the traditions of the country.

He was none of these things. Only a few years previously
he had been Emperor of France. He had known the glories
of the Tuileries Palace, liveried servants and carriages and
had led the armies of his nation into a disastrous war against
the Prussians. Moreover, he was the nephew of the terrible
Napoleon Bonaparte who had fought a bitter war against
Britain and had massed an army on the cliffs at Boulogne for
an invasion of Kent. Napoleon III was now in exile and had
come to Chislehurst where he and his empress and son, the
Prince Imperial, had been offered a refuge.

Louis Napoleon was no stranger to Chislehurst for he had
spent many years in England after Waterloo when the
Bourbons regained the throne of France and the Bonapartes
were chased out. He had always dreamed of succeeding to
his uncle's throne but it was many years before the opportunity arose. When he did get back as emperor he had an
uneasy eighteen years on the throne before being forced into
exile once more. He came back to England and it was
Camden Place at Chislehurst which was to be his home for
the few remaining years of his life.

Camden Place was first built by William Camden, the
headmaster of Westminster School and Clarenceaux King of
Arms. He lived in the house from 1609 to 1623. It was rebuilt
in 1700 and named Camden Place. It seems to have
remained in the Camden family during that century but in
1805 it was bought by a Mr Thomas Bonar. He and his wife
were the victims of a notorious murder in 1823 when they
were both killed by one of their servants. The murderer was
hanged in public on Penenden Heath outside Maidstone.

Camden Place then went to Henry Rowles, builder of
Drury Lane Theatre, and it was through his daughter Emily
that the connection with Louis Napoleon first started. The
young prince was in London and met Emily at the Drury
Lane Theatre. They became friends and Louis Napoleon was
a frequent visitor to her father's house at Chislehurst. It
would appear that she was taken into his confidence
regarding his plans to take the throne of France for she was
later to give him active assistance when he was in trouble.

Louis Napoleon badly misjudged the feelings of the French
people in believing that they wanted the return of the
Bonapartes. He attempted a *coup d'état* which was easily
defeated, and he was himself captured and imprisoned in the
Castle of Ham. Emily Rowles sent him letters and parcels
from Chislehurst with such frequency that the guards accepted them as routine and did not bother to examine them.
One parcel contained workmen's clothing. Louis Napoleon
put this on, walked out of the gate down to the railway
station and got on a train into Belgium. From there he
returned to England.

At this point something went wrong with the relationship
between Louis Napoleon and Emily. She had provided the
means for him to escape and he should have been duly
grateful, but they broke off contact. Did she hope one day to
become Empress of France and he rejected her as not being
suitable? Did her family forbid her to continue to assist a
foreigner on English soil to plot against a friendly nation?
The reason is not known but from the moment of his return
they lost contact with each other.

In 1848 Louis Napoleon went back to France when the
Orleanist reign was overthrown in a revolution. A republic
was declared and he was elected president. Two years later
he seized complete power and proclaimed himself Emperor
Napoleon III in 1852.

Meanwhile the Rowles family had moved from Camden
Place and it had been bought by Nathaniel Strode, a Fran-
cophil who set about transforming it into a French *château*.
From the Château de Bercy in France he brought over
panelling, doors and hinges which can still be seen in the
dining-room today. He also bought the wrought-iron gates
which had stood at the entrance to the Paris Exhibition of

1867. These remained at Camden Place until 1940 when they were removed and taken as scrap iron for the war effort. In 1870 the Franco-Prussian War broke out. Napoleon was at the head of his armies but suffered a crushing defeat at Sedan where he was captured by the Prussians. The Empress Eugénie fled by ship to Ryde on the Isle of Wight and her son, the Prince Imperial, was sent to Belgium. Nathaniel Strode then informed the imperial family that they could make their home at Camden Place. He moved out and Eugénie and the Prince Imperial moved in on 20 September 1870. Napoleon was released from captivity in the following March and rejoined his family at Camden Place.

The house then became the centre for Bonapartists. The emperor held court and he and Eugénie gave audiences. Among those who attended were the Prime Minister, William Gladstone, and the Archbishop of Canterbury.

Queen Victoria had always been on good terms with the French royal family and she and the Prince of Wales (later Edward VII) paid visits to Camden Place. Napoleon and Eugénie entered into the life of this English suburb. They attended Mass each Sunday at St Mary's Roman Catholic Church, presented prizes at local athletic meetings and held garden parties on the lawns. A cutting from a willow tree which grew over the grave of Napoleon on St Helena was planted in the grounds.

Napoleon III died at Camden Place on 9 June 1873. His funeral hearse was drawn by eight black horses and attended by members of the British royal family, French marshals and generals. He was buried in the mausoleum attached to St Mary's Church.

The Prince Imperial was determined to follow the military profession and was a student at the Royal Military Academy at Woolwich. When he came of age in 1874 the empress gave a big party for him in the grounds of Camden Place where he was toasted as 'Napoleon IV'. He succeeded in getting posted to South Africa for the Zulu War, despite the wishes of his mother. There he was caught in an ambush and speared to death. His body was brought home to Camden Place and he was buried beside his father. The pall bearers were the Prince of Wales and the royal Dukes of Cambridge, Edinburgh and Connaught.

Empress Eugénie lived on at Camden Place and endeavoured to make Chislehurst a shrine of the Bonapartes. She tried to found a Roman Catholic Abbey but the Protestant owner of the land refused to sell it for this purpose. Eventually she bought land at Farnborough, Hampshire, where she founded St Michael's Abbey. The bodies of Napoleon and the Prince Imperial were removed from Chislehurst to Farnborough and Eugénie left Camden Place for the last time in 1881.

Nathaniel Strode resumed occupation but, years later, Camden Place has become a golf club. The talk in the rooms of Camden Place is now of the royal and ancient game. A hundred years ago it concerned the chances of the Bonapartes regaining the imperial throne of France.

Camden Place is an impressive red and yellow brick building with a clock over the centre doorway and a skyline of stone balustrades. Much of the interior is as it was in Napoleon's day.

Over the border into Kent proper is the village of Sutton-at-Hone on the banks of the River Darent. It was here that one of the great religious military orders, the Sovereign or Military Order of the Knights Hospitaller of Saint John of Jerusalem, established one of their headquarters.

The Knights Hospitaller had their origin in a hospital attached to the church of St John the Baptist in Jerusalem following the capture by the crusaders in 1099. They were dedicated to the task of tending the sick and the poor and of waging war upon Islam. Crusader knights, who had been cared for and had their wounds healed, gratefully made gifts to the Order so that it became a wealthy and powerful body. It spread into every country of the Western world and took a leading part in the crusades. From their great castles at Marquat and the Krak des Chevaliers, they held the Moslems at bay and were the leading force which enabled King Richard I to achieve victory at Arsuf. When driven out of the Holy Land they moved to Cyprus in order to be near at hand for the reconquest.

The grand master of the Order was elected for life and ruled a celibate brotherhood of knights, serving brothers and chaplains. They owned considerable estates in all countries and each unit contributed one third of its revenues to its army and its hospital.

Malta was given to the Order as its headquarters by the Emperor Charles V for the price of one falcon a year and the obligation to keep the Muslims out of Tripoli. This led to the famous siege by Suleiman the Magnificent in 1565 which the knights successfully repulsed. The hero of that siege was Jean de la Valette and the new capital of Malta was named Valetta in his honour.

The Order, and that of its great rival the Knights Templar, was very powerful in this country in the Middle Ages and owned vast estates. The manor at Sutton-at-Hone was given to the Order by Robert Basing in 1212. A commandery was established and it became a training college for newly joined knights before going out to the crusades. As was the fate of other religious communities, it was suppressed by Henry VIII who presented it to a local landowner Sir Maurice Denys. The knights left and went to France, but some came back for a brief period when Mary I was on the throne. The buildings had started to decay and when the historian Edward Hasted took it over in 1757 he was faced with heavy repairs. He spent so much money on St John's that he found he could no longer afford to live there. His enthusiasm was to cost him dearly for the bills had not been paid and he was arrested for debt.

St John's Jerusalem is now in the care of the National Trust. The Great Chapel of flint and rubble still stands but the domestic buildings have gone. Great cedar and beech trees overhang the gardens which are contained by the twisting arms of the river. It is strange to think that this peaceful spot was once a battle-training ground, where knights charged at each other with levelled lances and learned to evade the slashes of the scimitars used by the Saracens.

2

The Valley of the Darent

THE RIVER DARENT flows north from the Sevenoaks area. It cannot be called a great river either in length or in width and yet it passes some of the most interesting historical places in the county. As a stream, it is within sight of a palace of the archbishops of Canterbury, it flows beside a fine Roman villa which has been its companion for nearly 2,000 years and on past a grim Norman castle. It then creeps through Dartford and out to the Thames below Erith.

Eynsford Castle, just off the main road, was neglected for many years but has now been restored by the Department of the Environment. This is a genuine castle, built for defence and not for show.

The term 'castle' has been much abused and misunderstood. It should strictly be applied only to those buildings erected after the Norman Conquest. A castle was a fortress built by the king or a great lord and was part of the feudal system which the Normans brought to this country. Nevertheless, the term has been used to take in the earthen hill forts of the Ancient Britons (e.g. Maiden Castle in Dorset) down to fairly modern manor houses.

The hill forts stormed by the Romans can hardly be described as 'castles', nor can the huge stone barracks erected by the Romans. The Normans were the great builders of castles and studded the county with them to overawe and keep at bay the defeated Saxons. For them defence was the first priority with comfort and living conditions a poor second.

Gunpowder spelt the end of the great age of castles for their walls could not stand up to battering from artillery. Fortifications, such as the 'castles' erected by Henry VIII along the south coast, would have to be stronger and smaller and slightly below the surface like those of the French Maginot Line. There are also the fortified manor houses with mock battlements which glory in the name of 'castle'. They would be as incapable of resisting a medieval siege as a modern council house.

But Eynsford is a real Norman castle, built shortly after the Conquest. The site had always belonged to the archbishops of Canterbury. In Domesday Book it is shown as belonging to the archbishop and held by a knight called Ralph. He founded a family which took the name of Eynsford. The castle was built by his son, the first William de Eynsford. It was a watch tower on a mound surrounded by a thick curtain wall. William was a sheriff of Kent and could read and write, a rare accomplishment for a knight in those days. He ended his days as a monk of Christ Church, Canterbury, and his son, another William, took over the castle in 1135.

It was this William who built the great hall which can still be seen and also considerably heightened the curtain wall. The castle was therefore a strong defence work and useful place of refuge during the civil wars which broke out in the reign of King Stephen. His son, yet another William, added more buildings, including the kitchen. He was still a liege of the Archbishop of Canterbury and there is a record of this William de Eynsford standing surety to the king on behalf of Archbishop Thomas Becket for the huge sum of 100 marks, probably amounting to more than £1,200 in modern currency.

A quarrel with Becket led to William leaving the castle. Becket appointed a priest to Eynsford who was not acceptable to William. The priest was forbidden to enter the church and William was promptly excommunicated by Becket. King Henry II interceded and ordered Becket to rescind the excommunication, which he did reluctantly. The breach was never properly healed and only ended with the murder of Becket in Canterbury Cathedral. William left Eynsford and died at Canterbury.

In the reign of King John, a grandson, also William, distinguished himself in the Irish wars and was in favour at court. However, when the barons rebelled against the king, William de Eynsford joined them and was captured when

King John successfully besieged Rochester Castle. The king wanted to hang the whole garrison but agreed to hold the knights to ransom. After the king's death, William recovered his lands and served as a royal seneschal to Henry III. His grandson inherited the property but the family line died out in 1261 with the death of his son, another William and the seventh to hold the castle of Eynsford.

Eynsford Castle passed through several hands and was for a time left unoccupied. While empty it was sacked. Doors were ripped off, windows smashed and goods stolen. The owner, William Inge, a judge, brought an action for damages against "certain persons including Nicholas de Criol". It seems that Nicholas de Criol was a descendant of a sister of the fifth William de Eynsford and considered he had a right to the property. A compromise settlement was reached but the court ruled that Criol, by inheritance, had certain rights to the castle. This did the Criols little good for they supported the Lancastrian cause in the Wars of the Roses and were executed by the victorious Yorkists.

The castle was used as a courthouse and later as hunting kennels but was never again occupied as a residence. It fell into decay but was rescued at the beginning of the twentieth century by the then owner who carried out some preservation work. It then went to the Society for the Protection of Ancient Buildings and to the Department of the Environment in 1948.

There is sufficient left standing to obtain an impression of the strength of the castle. The great curtain wall is almost intact, standing 30 feet in height and 6 feet thick. It is built of flint rubble with cement which has withstood the weather of 900 years. The great hall, which had to be rebuilt in 1250 after a fire, contains Roman tiles which probably came from the many Roman sites in the Darent valley.

Not far away and standing on the bank of the river, is one of the finest Roman villas discovered in this country. There is evidence of considerable occupation in Roman times along the valley which is a fertile area but the excavation of the Lullingstone Roman villa enabled an intriguing glimpse to be made into the lives of the inhabitants. Their mode of life, their religions, art and customs, and agricultural pursuits became clear as the archaeologists carefully shifted the earth and went back to the days of the Roman occupation.

Its discovery was accidental for the villa had been abandoned and lay under the accumulation of thirteen centuries of earth and debris which had covered it. A deer fence was being erected at the end of Lullingstone Park and when the holes for the reception of the timber posts were dug, part of a mosaic floor was uncovered. This was in the 1750s and strangely no notice was taken of it, apart from a reference in a book by an antiquary in 1788.

In 1949 a systematic excavation was undertaken and it was found that the villa was virtually untouched since it had been abandoned following a fire at the start of the fifth century. Clay and flint which had been washed down the hillside towards the river covered the villa and preserved many of the walls upright, a rather rare feature because with most Roman villas only the foundations are left.

As excavation proceeded it could be seen that the villa and its temples were a prominent group of buildings above the river. The house was a large bungalow with a wooden framework standing on a foundation of flint and mortar. It was finished with daub and coated with plaster painted with highly coloured designs. It had a red-tiled roof.

The dining and reception rooms had magnificent mosaic floors and were lighted by glazed windows high up in the walls. Leading off at the end were the baths which are always a feature of any Roman establishment. At the other end was a deep room which served a number of purposes and over this was a private Christian chapel, the first to have been found in this country. Behind the house was a pagan temple - mausoleum capped by a pink dome. To the south were a granary and other farm buildings.

The villa was occupied for more than 300 years. It was the centre of a farming community where corn was grown and the woodlands provided beech mast for the pigs and fuel for heating purposes. The buildings were probably erected with the aid of Roman army technicians for they were well constructed. By the end of the second century A.D. the owners were apparently wealthy for the bathing apartments were built and room added for the cult worship of pagan gods. Tiled stairs were put in to lead down to these rooms and the old farmhouse had now been transformed into a country house with all the latest modern conveniences. The new owner was probably an important Roman official for he brought over marble busts of his ancestors to decorate the rooms. His high-quality pottery for use by the household included Samian ware, drinking cups with hunting scenes and fine cups and vases from the Rhineland. He also had the thatch taken off the roof and replaced by red tiles.

The baths were laid out in the usual Roman style with the cold room leading to the tepid room, on to the hot room and back to the large cold plunge room. The water supply came from a well which is still fed by a pure spring. The deep room was devoted to the worship of the local water goddesses, paintings of whom can still be seen on the walls.

This wealthy Roman had occupied the villa for about twenty years when something happened which caused him and his family to abandon it in a hurry. His marble busts were left behind and there is evidence that it was a hasty evacuation which had not been planned in advance. If it had been a local war or political upheaval which sent him and his family packing, it was apparently soon over. Some local people took over and used the kitchens as a tannery. Two pits were dug, one for washing the leather and the other for tanning. Leather boots and sandals and what appears to be the smith's leather apron were found in these pits.

The tanner and his family eventually left and the villa remained empty for more than fifty years. A Romano-British farming family then moved in and commenced some much-needed repairs. The baths were rebuilt, a large granary erected and the marble busts of the previous owner put into the deep room which seems to have taken on the duties of a pagan temple, a store-room and an attic.

The granary, 80 feet long, was built with flint and mortar and had a thatched roof. Paw marks of dogs have been found in the mortar as they walked on it before it was set. Behind the house the new occupier erected a pagan temple – mausoleum designed for the burial of a young man and a young woman. Their bodies were enclosed in lead coffins and glass bottles, flagons, bowls, knives, spoons and other items which they might have needed in another world were buried with them, together with a square gaming board and a set of thirty pieces, fifteen white and fifteen red. It would have been for a game of draughts or for some form of backgammon.

About this period the splendid mosaic floors were laid. The floor in the reception room has the typical Roman four seasons in the corners. Spring is represented by a young girl who has a swallow perching on her shoulder, autumn is an older woman with corn in her hair, and winter is an old woman wearing a hood over her head. Summer is missing as this is the spot where the stake for the deer fence was driven in. The centre panel has dolphins gambolling round the border and Bellerophon mounted upon the winged horse Pegasus driving a spear into the monster, Chimaera. In the dining-room is a mosaic floor depicting the abduction of Europa by the god Jupiter who had transformed himself into a white bull. In the mosaic, the bull is shown swimming through the water accompanied by two Cupids. These mosaic floors in red and white are among the finest discovered anywhere in this country. Other parts of the mosaic floor have crosses, leaves, hearts, squares and other designs including, rather strangely, some striking swastikas reminiscent of Hitler's Germany.

Around the middle of the fourth century A.D. this wealthy farmer and his family embraced Christianity. Over the deep room, which still contained the marble busts and votive pots, a room was converted to a chapel. The walls were decorated with a row of human figures in the attitude of prayer and a large Christian monogram painted at the entrance. Pagan worship continued below in the deep room and Christian worship in the chapel above. It is probable that the Lullingstone chapel was used to attract more converts to the Christian faith for the entrance room could be used by those under instruction or possible recruits to share in the services from a distance. This chapel is the only example in this country of Christian worship being carried on within the walls of a Roman villa. One wonders if there was any antagonism between the followers of the old gods below and those of the new religion above. Not many years had elapsed since Christians were martyred in Rome and it was to be another 200 years before St Augustine arrived to convert the island to Christianity.

Early in the fifth century a disastrous fire severely damaged the buildings and the inhabitants left. The only casualty was their cat which died in the fire. They did not return to repair the building and, as no one else took it over, it was left to the earth to slip forward and bury it. Twelve years of careful excavation have now revealed it and enabled the archaeologists to piece together the fascinating story of its 500 years of existence. Here can be seen the baths, the deep room used for pagan worship, the wonderful mosaic floors and the Christian emblems painted on the walls. The marble busts have gone to the British Museum but casts of them are on display at Lullingstone. There were also coins, pottery, cups and dishes found together with the shells of oysters of which the Romans were so fond. The picture comes through of wealthy families enjoying life in this very pleasant villa beside the river.

The richest manor of the Archbishop of Canterbury once stood at Otford. Now there is little remaining except for a great red-brick octagonal tower which was one of those which stood at the corners of this huge palace.

There was a manor house here at the time of the Norman Conquest for Archbishop Lanfranc stayed in it on occasions. The site was presented to Canterbury Christ Church by King Offa of Mercia as a penance for the lives lost in his victory at the Battle of Otford in 773. Archbishop Wareham scrapped the manor house and built the palace in 1506. It was built in red brick, covered an area 440 feet by 220 feet, and was two storeys high. Tall towers stood at the corners and entry was through a great gatehouse. Inside were two large courtyards. It is not known how many rooms it contained but when the palace was surveyed in 1573 it was reported that 200 door keys were missing.

It must have been able to cope with large numbers of visitors for it is recorded that Archbishop Wareham entertained Cardinal Campeggio and his 1,000 retainers at Otford. Later, on his way to the Field of the Cloth of Gold, Henry VIII turned up with 4,000 and his queen, Katherine of Aragon, with another 1,000 followers. Apart from finding room for them within the palace, the problem of feeding such a large company must have been formidable, particularly with the huge meals which the Tudors expected. Archbishop Thomas Becket was often at Otford where he greatly improved the buildings of the old manor house. William Lambarde, whose *Perambulation of Kent* was published in 1570, speaks of the "spiteful miracles" performed by Becket at Otford. (Lambarde was a staunch Protestant and wrote scathingly of the Roman Catholic Church in England before the Reformation.) He refers to the building operations being conducted by Becket at Otford when there was a lack of water. Becket stuck his staff into the ground and water came up from a spring. This would have seemed a not too difficult miracle to perform for a small stream runs across the ground and Henry VIII complained that "Otford standeth too low and is rheumatick like unto Croydon". The other two "spiteful miracles" were the banishment of birds from Otford after the song of a nightingale had disturbed the archbishop's devotions, and the expulsion of blacksmiths after one had injured his horse.

Otford Palace was ceded to Henry VIII by Archbishop Cranmer. The king was often in Kent when visiting Anne Boleyn at Hever Castle and told Cranmer that he wanted Otford as well as Knole which was also owned by the archbishops of Canterbury. Cranmer wanted to retain Knole for himself and suggested that the king could be content with Otford. Henry then referred to the palace as standing "low and is rheumatick like unto Croydon where I could never be without sickness". So the king took both places and remarked, "I will live at Knole and most of my house shall live at Otford."

Henry soon lost interest in Otford and within ten years it needed repairs. It was surveyed in the reign of Edward VI when it was reported that "the great hall is in great decay in default of lead, timber and stone work is fallen down and glass windows are broken". Repairs were estimated at £106. Nothing seems to have been done for by 1573 another survey put the cost of repairs at £1,600. By 1596 its state was much worse for "it stands in a very wet soil upon springs and vents of water are continually coming up under it and the floors and walls are hoary and musty". Elizabeth I sold the place in 1601 for £2,000 to pay for her Irish wars.

Various owners included the Sidneys of Penshurst and

William Pitt, but little was done to the buildings which were
falling down. In 1790 the palace and grounds were auctioned
and fetched £20,128. It was cut up into lots. One of these was
shown as "The ruins of the ancient palace of Otford" and
another as "Becket's Well Piece".

The massive Tudor tower still stands as a reminder of past
glories. Becket's miracles do not seem to have survived into
the twentieth century. Birds nest in the tower of the palace
and a blacksmith is still in business. There are, however,
traces of his well in the wet fields in which one can sink up
to the ankles.

Chevening, at the foot of the hill on the other side of the
motorway, is to be the home of Prince Charles. It had been
in the Stanhope family for nearly 250 years before the death
of the last earl in 1967 when it was left to the nation with
£250,000 for its upkeep.

The house was built in 1616 to a design by Inigo Jones for
Earl Dacre. In 1721 it was bought by James Stanhope, one
of the Duke of Marlborough's generals, for £28,000. He made
extensive additions and refaced it with stone and coloured
tiles. He died suddenly in 1721 after making a violent speech
in the House of Lords about the South Sea Bubble scandal.

The third earl, Charles Stanhope, was a strong supporter
of the French Revolution and was known as 'Citizen
Stanhope'. He became chairman of the Revolution Society
and withdrew from the House of Lords. Before he died in
1816 he disinherited all his children.

One of his daughters was to achieve even greater notoriety.
Lady Hester Stanhope became the housekeeper and trusted
confidant of her uncle, William Pitt, the prime minister. On
his death she left England, made a pilgrimage to Jerusalem
and camped with the Bedouins in the desert. She settled on
Mount Lebanon where she adopted Eastern dress and habits
and held court amongst the Arabs. She died, a deserted
eccentric, at the age of sixty-three.

Since the death of the last earl, Chevening has been
neglected but work is going on to restore the gardens, lake
and park. The park was enclosed in 1792 and blocks the old
Pilgrims' Way which has had to be rerouted around the
edges.

3

Around the Sevenoaks Area

THE VILLAGE OF WESTERHAM nestling beneath the Downs is connected with two famous men separated by a gap of 200 years.

It was here that General James Wolfe was born and spent his early years and it was here that he was presented with his first commission in the British Army. A fine statue of Wolfe flourishing his sword stands on the village green.

The other was Sir Winston Churchill who bought Chartwell Manor in 1922. It was to remain his home for the next forty years in peace and in war, in office and on the back benches. Many famous people visited him there and discussed international problems far into the night. It was at Chartwell that he wrote his great historical works, *The World Crisis, Marlborough* and the *History of the Second World War*. He has left his mark on Chartwell in the shape of the walls which he built with his own hands and the lake with its island which he constructed.

James Wolfe, who could claim indirect descent on his mother's side from King Edward III, was born into a military family. His grandfather was a major in a foot regiment and his father a lieutenant-colonel in a regiment of marines. The Wolfes moved to Westerham in 1726 and rented a house called Spiers which has now been renamed Quebec House. On 2 January 1727 James Wolfe was born at Westerham Vicarage where Mrs Wolfe was staying during the absence of her husband with his regiment.

The Wolfes remained in Westerham until 1738 when they moved to Greenwich but the family continued to visit their friends in the village. James Wolfe was, in fact, at Westerham when a courier from Whitehall handed him his first commission as a second-lieutenant in his father's regiment.

He was only fourteen at the time but, three years later, he was adjutant of the 12th Regiment of Foot when it took part in the Battle of Dettigen. At this battle the British Army was commanded by George II, the last occasion on which a British sovereign led his troops into battle. Wolfe had his horse shot from under him but continued on foot.

In 1745 he was in Scotland with Butcher Cumberland's army facing the Highland clans under Bonnie Prince Charlie. At the Battle of Culloden he offered to resign his commission after he had refused to shoot a wounded Highlander but, although he was now out of favour, he continued in his regiment. His later service included spells in Holland and Ireland and on the abortive expedition to Rochefort. He was promoted to colonel in the face of opposition from his superiors who described him as most unreliable. George II was impressed with his energy and, approving the promotion, said: "Mad is he? Then I hope he will bite some other of my generals."

Wolfe was next in action in French Canada where he won new laurels by his storming of the fortress at Louisberg. He came home to England and went to Bath to take the waters as a cure for gravel and rheumatism. Before he had completed his cure he was sent for and ordered to take command of the force going up the St Lawrence to attack Quebec. His exploits – scaling the Heights of Abraham and his great victory – are an essential part of British history. He was ill throughout the battle, was wounded twice in the early stages but carried on until, with victory assured, a third shot killed him.

Wolfe's body was brought back to England and buried in the parish church at Greenwich. His defeated opponent, the Marquis de Montcalm, is also remembered in Westerham where a restaurant has been named after him.

Quebec House, now owned by the National Trust, is built of brick and Kentish ragstone. A panel bears the arms of Henry VII and there is some evidence that the house dates back to the fifteenth century although it has been much restored. It was a Canadian owner, Joseph Bowles Learmont of Montreal, who had the house presented to the National Trust on his death in 1918.

There are many objects connected with James Wolfe

preserved in Quebec House. These include paintings of him as a young man, his fight at Quebec and his death. His snuff box, dressing-gown, telescope and his travelling canteen containing griddle, frying-pan, condiment set and glass decanters are displayed together with the Wolfe Family Bible. A collection of arms used by his soldiers in the campaigns comprises muskets, halberds and the hangers or short swords carried by the troops of the line.

The other house in Westerham connected with Wolfe is Squerryes Court which has been in the ownership of the Warde family for nearly 250 years. Wolfe was a great friend of the Wardes and it was in the garden of Squerryes that he received his first commission from the hands of the Whitehall courier. A cenotaph on this spot was erected shortly after Wolfe's death in 1759. The house is on a site owned by a family named de Squerie from 1216 until 1463. The old house was pulled down and completely rebuilt by its owner, Sir Nicholas Crisp, in 1680 and it passed into the hands of the Warde family in 1731. A room in the house devoted to mementoes of Wolfe displays the sword he wore at Quebec.

Over the hill, crowned in early summer with rhododendrons and in a glorious position overlooking the Weald of Kent, is Chartwell, also owned by the National Trust. The estate was originally called Atwell after the first owner who had a farmhouse there in 1352.

It passed through many hands until it was bought by John Colquhoun in 1848. He spent large sums of money on rebuilding and finally transformed the old farmhouse into a country mansion. The estate remained in the Colquhoun family for the next seventy years but in 1921 Major Campbell Colquhoun put it up for auction. The reserve price was not reached and it was withdrawn. Sir Winston Churchill then stepped in and bought the estate for £5,000. This was surely one of the greatest bargains of all time in house purchase for the timber on the estate alone was valued at £2,000.

Churchill had entered Parliament in 1900 as Conservative MP for Oldham but went over to the Liberals four years later. By 1908 he was in the Cabinet and was First Lord of the Admiralty when war broke out in 1914. The failure of the Dardanelles expedition led to his removal from this post but he returned later as Minister for Munitions. Shortly after he had bought Chartwell he lost his seat in the House of Commons but returned later having left the Liberals and joined the Conservative Party again.

With the defeat of the Conservative Government in 1929 Churchill was out of office and remained outside as a back bencher until recalled, again as First Lord of the Admiralty, upon the outbreak of the Second World War in 1939. It was during this period that he devoted his time and energies to his family, his writing and to Chartwell.

The house was completely transformed from a dark, ivy-clad building into a modern country home at a cost of nearly £20,000. The front was remodelled and another wing added. The interior was gutted and completely rebuilt.

It was also the grounds and the garden which received Churchill's attention. Trees were brought in and planted and he laid out strawberry and asparagus beds. With his own hands he built the brick wall surrounding the kitchen garden and much of a small cottage. Rockeries were constructed and one wall was modelled on a wall at Quebec House where Wolfe lived.

Churchill had a passion for what he termed his water-works. He made a bathing pool, divided the bottom lakes with a dam and made an island in the middle. The stream which runs down the slope was a great attraction to the statesman and out of it he constructed waterfalls and rock pools. Some were made into fish pools and were stocked with golden orfe which would come to the edge to be fed. On the lakes he encouraged waterfowl including the famous black swans which were a gift from Australia.

The house contains a host of objects associated with the life of the ninety-year-old soldier, journalist, author, painter, politician and statesman. It was bought by friends of Churchill who presented it to the National Trust and therefore preserved much as it was in his lifetime. Here are the family portraits and a painting of Blenheim Palace where he was born in 1874.

A connection with Chislehurst and Napoleon III is a set of china used by the emperor in his palace at the Tuileries. The palace was gutted in the Commune rising of 1871 but, before it was burned down, there was an auction of its contents in the street. Sir Winston's grandmother was in Paris and went along to the auction where she bought the china, packed it on a wheelbarrow and took it back to her hotel.

Churchill's many uniforms are on display. These include those of an Elder Brother of Trinity House, Lord Warden of the Cinque Ports, Royal Air Force, Privy Councillor, Chancellor of Bristol University, and his famous siren suit which he wore in the Second World War.

His standard as Lord Warden hangs from the roof together with a replica of his banner as a Knight of the Garter. The first Allied flag to be flown in a captured enemy capital during the war is also here. It was hoisted over Rome when it was captured on 5 June 1944. Other souvenirs from the war include a model of the Mulberry Harbour which was used on the Normandy invasion beaches and gifts from Stalin and General De Gaulle.

The visitors' book contains the signatures of practically every great man of the time. One of the last to sign was Field-Marshal Viscount Montgomery who visited Chartwell in October 1964, three months before Churchill's death.

In his studio in the garden are Churchill's easel and paint box and his paintings, some uncompleted at the time of his death. Most of these are landscapes which were a favourite subject of the painter. Over the door is the head of a fighting bull killed by the famous Spanish matador Manolete on VE Day 1945. It has a white V on its forehead.

Chartwell is not just a collection of objects in a museum. Churchill did not have to wait for years after his death to be proclaimed a famous man. Upon his death the contents of the house were preserved as he had known and used them and this gives the visitor the feeling of actually being in the place at the time that the great man was living there. Sir Walter Scott's home at Abbotsford has this same quality. The quill pen he was using when he died is there on the desk where he left it. At Chartwell the half-squeezed tubes of paint lie there waiting for the painter to pick them up again and complete the canvas. It was at Westminster that Churchill worked but it is here at Chartwell that he lived.

Knole, just south of Sevenoaks, is one of the great stately homes of England. Standing on a knoll, from which it takes its name, it is a huge establishment mainly built of grey Kentish ragstone with roofs of reddish-brown tiles. Some idea of its size may be gained from the fact that it has seven courtyards (one for every day of the week), fifty-two staircases (one for every week of the year) and 365 rooms (one for every day of the year). These mathematics were not, however, intended when it was built, for Knole has grown from what was probably once a humble farmhouse to the huge palace which the visitor sees today. Successive owners were continually adding to the structure. It stands in a park six miles in circumference.

In its early days Knole is said to have been owned by the great families of Bethure, Pembroke and Bigod. In the reign of Edward I there is a record of a Robert de Knolle living there in a farmhouse. Later owners improved the building and in 1370 it was bought by Geoffrey Lord de Say. His great-grandson sold it to Thomas Bouchier, Archbishop of Canterbury, in 1456 for £266.

Bouchier was the first great builder at Knole, where he lived for thirty years. He transferred the rather uncomfortable collection of buildings into a palace fit for the great clerics of the Middle Ages. His work can still be seen in the main entrance and the great courtyard within. The building here has machiolations in the parapets but it is thought that these must have been added for decoration as it is unlikely that archbishops would have needed to use them for their real purpose of pouring boiling oil or water on to a besieging enemy force.

Knole was formally presented to the See of Canterbury by Bouchier before his death and four more archbishops, Morton, Deane, Wareham and Cranmer, were to hold and enjoy the estate. In Cranmer's time Henry VIII cast covetous eyes upon it and although, as we have seen, Cranmer tried to hold Knole and let the king have Otford, it passed into royal hands. Henry showed more respect for Knole than he did for Otford for he spent large sums of money repairing and improving it. His accounts show £872 for work in 1543 and £770 in 1548.

In 1551 Knole was presented to John Dudley, Duke of

Northumberland, but he apparently did not like it for he gave it back to the Crown within two years. For a brief period Knole returned to the archbishops for Queen Mary presented it to Cardinal Reginald Pole. Its next owner was Robert Dudley, Earl of Leicester, favourite of Queen Elizabeth I. He sub-let it to a family named Lennard and then gave it back to the queen who gave it to her cousin, Thomas Sackville, in 1566. This started the Sackville ownership of Knole which continued up to modern times.

This Thomas Sackville could trace his ancestry back to the Lord of Sauquerville in Normandy before the Norman Conquest. His grandmother had been an aunt of Anne Boleyn and he was therefore related to Queen Elizabeth. He held high office during her reign being Lord High Treasurer, Lord High Steward, and was created Earl of Dorset. He often headed important embassies abroad. Having inherited a fortune from his father he spent huge sums on Knole. His accounts show payments for plasterers, upholsterers, glaziers and masons and the importing of 300 Italian labourers. He also had his own private orchestra.

His son survived for only one year at Knole but the next earl, Richard, is described as a family disaster. He was a noted gambler who sold his property in London and other estates for £80,000, mortgaged Knole and was £60,000 in debt when he died. He attempted to get his hands on his wife's fortune but she refused to give it up to him.

A brother succeeded as the fourth earl and by careful management he started to make good the depredations of the previous holder when the Civil War broke out. Supporting the royalist cause, he had his goods seized by the parliamentary troops who raided Knole. When Parliament set up its county committees, Knole was selected as the headquarters for Kent. The Dorset estates were sequestered and the contents of the house were sold. The war had cost the Sackvilles more than £40,000.

Richard Sackville, the fifth earl, married an heiress and her money helped to restore Knole to its former glory. His son, Charles, who succeeded him in 1677, was a great favourite at the court of Charles II. One of his mistresses was Nell Gwynne who always referred to him as 'Charles the First'. He was a great literary figure and a friend of Dryden and Pope. He spent his last years sadly at Bath dominated by his third wife who "kept him in a sort of captivity".

The seventh earl, Lionel, was sent to Hanover to announce to George I that Queen Anne had died and was rewarded with a dukedom. His grandson, the third Duke of Dorset, was renowned as a cricketer and was ambassador in France when the French Revolution broke out in 1789.

With the death of the fifth duke in 1843 the title became extinct and Knole went to an aunt who married George West, the Earl de la Warr. Their children assumed the names of Sackville-West but in 1876 a descendant was created Lord Sackville. In 1946 Knole was handed over to the National Trust.

The house shows plenty of evidence of its changes of ownership. The leaden heads of drainpipes in one of the courtyards bear the initials "T.D. 1605". The Great Hall was built by Archbishop Bouchier in 1460 with a minstrels' gallery pierced by lattice holes. The steel fire-dogs bear the arms of Henry VIII and of Anne Boleyn. In the King's Bedroom is a silver and gold bed reputed to have cost £8,000 when it was put in for a visit by King James I. At the foot of a staircase is a nude reclining figure of Gianette Baccelli, the Italian mistress of the third duke, the cricketer, who is said to have had an affair with Marie Antoinette when he was in Paris. When he died this statue was stowed away in an attic where it would not be seen, but it has now been moved back to its original position.

Knole is a treasure house of furniture and paintings. There are great Elizabethan armchairs, Queen Anne stools, Brussels tapestries and a Charles I billiards table. Much of this furniture was collected from royal places by the sixth earl. Practically every painter of note is represented, including Van Dyck, Reynolds, Holbein, Rembrandt, Sir Peter Lely and Gainsborough.

The deer park is over 1,000 acres in extent. The gardens cover 26 acres and most of them were laid out in the reign of Charles I.

Knole is a very large place and the visitor must not expect to rush round it in a half-hour. There is also so much to absorb of this establishment with 500 years of history behind it that many people find a return visit necessary.

On the way to Ightham one might make a diversion to the Iron Age hill fort at Oldbury, just off the main road. This is a large camp of 120 acres rising to a height of 600 feet and dating from about 500 B.C. It was fortified against the Romans but they seem to have experienced little difficulty in overcoming it. At the sides are rock shelters cut into the hill which provided some form of rough dwelling for the defenders. It has a single rampart and ditch which can be clearly identified. After the Roman invasion it seems to have been completely abandoned and is now pleasantly covered with oak, beech and birch trees.

Ightham Mote, which is privately owned but open on certain days, should not be missed. In the idyllic surroundings of wooded hills is this delightful moated medieval manor house which has no rival in this country. The grey stone walls are reflected in the moat where swans swim. On the banks are beautiful peacocks, while white doves fly in and out of their ancient dovecot.

One is almost tempted to wonder if Ightham Mote is as good as it looks. Surely it must have been heavily restored in Victorian times or possibly built in a mock-Tudor style in this century. It is, however, quite genuine and has been looking like this for the past 500 years.

It also has two mysteries. A seated female skeleton was found behind a bricked-up door. It is not known who she was or what she had done. Was it a deliberate callous murder, or had she taken refuge behind the door and, being unable to get out again, died there years before the door was sealed up? There is an echo of the Gunpowder Plot at Ightham. The letter to Lord Monteagle warning him to stay away from Parliament which would receive a "terrible blow" was deciphered by the lady of the manor. The letter, badly written and deliberately vague in content, came into the hands of Dame Dorothy Selby who worked out its true meaning. As a result the cellars under Westminster were searched and Guy Fawkes was caught red-handed. How the letter came into her possession is unknown but Ightham was always a Catholic house and would not have wanted a leading Catholic peer to lose his life. Possibly a friend of the Selbys wrote it and had it passed on through the Selby family. Whatever happened it seems clear that the letter meant nothing to the authorities until Dame Dorothy deciphered it.

Ightham Mote (the name means 'a meeting place') was built early in the fourteenth century as a fortified manor house, not to withstand a medieval siege but to keep out wandering bands of brigands and robbers. It was held by Sir Thomas Cawne in 1340 and then passed to the de Haut family in 1370. This family were relatives of the Woodvilles, one of whom, Elizabeth, was married to Edward IV. When Richard III took the throne he found the Woodvilles plotting against him and so the de Hauts were thrown out of Ightham. With the defeat of Richard at Bosworth Field they got back their property.

In the reign of Queen Elizabeth, the Selby family were the owners and were to remain there for nearly 300 years. Dame Dorothy, who died in 1641, was a renowned needlewoman and her monument in Ightham church states, "She was a Dorcas whose curious needle turned the abused stage of this lewd world into the golden age".

Through the fourteenth-century doorway can be seen the Great Hall, 30 feet long, 20 feet wide and 38 feet high with its original oak roof timbers and corbels. The hall was panelled in 1872 when the doorway was uncovered and the skeleton found behind it. A suit of Cromwellian armour was found in the moat, probably abandoned at the time of the Restoration. There are two chapels, one of the fourteenth century and the other constructed in Tudor times with a painted barrel roof. Above this is a belfry and a single-handed seventeenth-century clock.

Ightham Mote is a priceless piece of medieval Kent preserved intact for the twentieth century to enjoy. Few such places have escaped the ravages of time or the enthusiastic vandalism of the restorer, but Ightham is one of these.

Although not an historic building, it is worth making a detour to see the quintain on the village green at Offham for it is the only one in the country. This is a relic of the days when knights needed to practise to keep their horses in good fettle and to perfect their marksmanship with the lance. The quintain is a tall post with a swivelling cross-piece at the top.

One end of this cross-piece, pierced with small holes, was the target and from the other end was hung a bag of sand. The idea of the game was to charge at it with levelled lance, hit the target and move smartly on before the heavy bag of sand swung round and knocked the knight off his horse. This simulated the attack on an enemy, a hit on his body and a swift manoeuvre to avoid his counter-stroke. The legend says that "he that by chance hit it not at all was treated with loud peals of derision, and he who did hit it made the best use of his swiftness lest he should have a sound blow on his neck from the bag of sand which instantly swung round from the other end of the quintain".

4

Along the Sussex Border

THIS PART OF KENT running along the border into Sussex is described by many people as the loveliest part of the county—a claim which would be disputed by those who live in the Weald, the Darent and Medway villages, and in other areas. Nevertheless, it can claim some of the most glorious countryside studded with ancient castles and country homes. It also has the source of the River Medway, which divides the Men of Kent from the Kentish Men.

As this division is always a matter of some confusion to those not born or living in the county, it may be useful at this point to go back into history and give some of the background. Kent is the only one of the English counties to retain its earliest known name. When the Romans invaded they found it inhabited by a tribe called the Cantii which they latinized as Cantium. The Saxons called it Cantiguarlandt, the land of the Cantii, and in Domesday Book the Normans labelled it Chent. Shortly afterwards it was written as Kent.

The first kings of England were kings of Kent, starting with Hengist in A.D. 455. They continued as separate rulers until the county was absorbed into Wessex in 825 and therefore Kent has a just claim to being the oldest kingdom in the country. Hengist and Horsa landed in Thanet in A.D. 449 under their banner of the white horse and this has remained the county badge. It can be seen on the county arms, on regimental standards and badges, on maps, trade tokens, hip pockets and even on steam rollers.

The difference between the Men of Kent and the Kentish Men is explained by the Saxon settlements after their infiltration. They were invited into this county to repel the

The Queen's House at Greenwich

The Royal Naval College at Greenwich

The old Royal Observatory at Greenwich

The Royal Palace of Eltham

Hall Place, Bexley

Camden Place, Chislehurst, former home of the Emperor Napoleon III

Mosaic pavement in the Roman villa at Lullingstone

The ruins of the Archbishop's Palace at Otford

Quebec House, Westerham, former home of Wolfe of Quebec

Chartwell, home of Sir Winston Churchill

Knole, Sevenoaks, home of the Sackvilles

Below: Archbishop Bouchier's Court at Knole

Ightham Mote near Sevenoaks

The gatehouse of Tonbridge Castle

Chiddingstone Castle near Tonbridge

Below: The nude portrait of Nell Gwynne commissioned by King Charles II, at Chiddingstone Castle

Penshurst Place, home of the Sidneys

Hever Castle, former home of Anne Boleyn

The tower of Hadlow Castle

The Palladian Mereworth Castle

The pavilion in Mote Park, Maidstone, erected by Kentish Volunteers as a tribute to Lord Romney

Leeds Castle, near Maidstone, seen from the east

Allington Castle on the River Medway near Maidstone

The Friars, Aylesford, near Maidstone

Cobham Hall near Rochester, former home of the Darnleys

Upnor Castle on the River Medway near Rochester

The Norman keep of Rochester Castle

Right: Rochester Cathedral

Below: The twin towers of the gatehouse to Cooling Castle

The ruins of Scotney Castle, Lamberhurst

Sissinghurst Castle, restored by V. Sackville-West

Vikings and, once there, refused to leave. There were clashes between them and the Ancient Britons culminating in the Battle of Aylesford in A.D. 455 when the Britons were defeated and routed and Hengist assumed the crown of Kent. The Britons fled and left the county north and west of the River Medway deserted. Hengist and his men had settled in and colonized the area south and east of the Medway and later another Saxon tribe from the Frisian Islands moved into north-west Kent. They were quite distinct from the Saxons in south-east Kent and these separate identities were preserved for many years, being known as the East Centingas and the West Centingas. The tradition continues today in the county society, the Association of Men of Kent and Kentish Men, the largest county society in Britain. Those born east and south of the River Medway are Men of Kent and those born west and north are Kentish Men.

The River Medway actually has its source just over the border in Sussex near East Grinstead and enters the county of Kent near Tunbridge Wells where it is joined by the River Eden. By far the greater area lies to the south-east of the river, the land of the Men of Kent, but the population is about even as the London conurbation plus the towns of Sevenoaks, Gravesend and Dartford count against the more sparsely populated areas of east Kent.

By the time the Medway reaches Tonbridge it has become a sizable river. The main road from London to Hastings crosses it here and, at such an important river and road junction, it is natural to expect to find a castle guarding it. Tonbridge Castle was one of the first to be built by the Normans after the Conquest. Richard Fitzgilbert, who fought at the Battle of Hastings, was given the town of Tonbridge and the lowey (the area surrounding it) by William I, and built a castle on a prehistoric mound by the river. It was built of stone, and surrounded by a moat fed by the river.

When William II came to the throne in 1087 he faced a revolt led by the Conqueror's half-brother, Odo, Bishop of Bayeux, and Earl of Kent. They wanted Robert, the eldest son, to succeed and thus keep England and Normandy under one ruler. Richard Fitzgilbert joined the rebels and was at Tonbridge Castle when it was successfully besieged by

William II and his troops. He was severely wounded during the siege and surrendered the castle which had resisted for only two days.

Fortunate to escape with his life from the fiery king, Richard, who had now taken the surname of 'de Tonbridge' was sent to Normandy and held prisoner until death in 1091. It was sad end for a Norman knight who had fought gallantly at Hastings and had been one of the Conqueror's most trusted companions.

The castle passed into the hands of the de Clare family who built the magnificent gatehouse which still stands today. Gilbert de Clare joined Simon de Montfort in his rebellion against Henry III and Tonbridge Castle was again at war. It was captured by Henry and his army in 1264 when the town was burnt and suffered badly. Gilbert made amends by changing sides and fighting for the king at Evesham and then married the king's grand-daughter. A son-in-law inherited the property but he was another who backed the wrong side when he took part in a rebellion against Edward I and so lost the castle. It was restored to the family by Edward III.

During the Civil War the castle was held by the Parliamentarians and successfully withstood several attacks. It later fell into decay and much of the building had gone when it was bought by Thomas Hooker in 1793. He constructed the modern buildings along the old curtain wall which are now used as council offices. The great gatehouse with its drum towers has survived but the old bailey has now become a flower garden and lawn.

Tunbridge Wells is a comparative newcomer and owes its existence to the accidental discovery of the healing properties of its water in 1606. Lord North, a member of the court of James I, found himself, at the age of twenty-five slowly dying. He left London for a change of air and also to be away from the excesses of court life and stayed with friends at a hunting lodge at Eridge, an estate seven miles south of Tonbridge. His health did not improve so he rode back to London. On his way he noticed a stream which had a scum on it which reminded him of the healing waters at Spa where he had been on military service. He knelt down and tasted the water and then obtained bottles to take samples of the water back to London where they could be analysed. These tests were encouraging and so he went back to the stream where he drank the waters until he was completely recovered.

His completely unexpected cure was soon widely broadcast in London and attracted many more patients. The name and the fame of the wells near Tonbridge was now made. The area was cleared of scrub, wells were dug and a stone pavement laid. There was only one miserable cottage in the area and so the patients had to find lodgings in Tonbridge. When Henrietta Maria, queen of Charles I, visited the wells in 1630 she and her suite had to camp out on the downs.

By the time that the place was honoured by a second royal visit, by Catherine of Braganza, queen of Charles II, in 1663, the fashionable popularity of Tunbridge Wells was assured and it was soon to rival Bath as a health and social resort. This was achieved in 1735 when the famous Beau Nash was lured away from Bath to become Master of Ceremonies at Tunbridge Wells.

This was the zenith of the town's prosperity. In 1736 the company included seven dukes and duchesses, thirty-three marquises, earls and barons, the prime minister, members of parliament and army officers. In addition to the healing properties of the water, Nash provided orchestras, gaming halls, balls and libraries. Every new arrival at Tunbridge Wells was greeted by a peal of bells for which they paid one guinea if they were a member of the nobility and a half-guinea if they were commoners.

Queen Anne, before she came to the throne, was a frequent visitor. In 1698 she brought her ailing son, the Duke of Gloucester, to take the cure. He met with an accident when he stumbled and fell on the rough path and the Princess donated £100 for the walks to be paved. When she came back the work had not been completed and she vowed never to return to Tunbridge Wells again. She kept her word and favoured Bath in future years. The work was soon completed, however, and the promenade and entrance square were paved with pantiles, curved roofing squares, some of which are still in evidence.

Very few people now come to Tunbridge Wells to take the

waters but the town retains the air of elegance of a bygone age. The spring of chalybeate water bubbles up into the well at the entrance to the Pantiles, an elegant promenade, and it needs little imagination to conjure up the scene as it was in the days when Beau Nash ruled this spa.

Chiddingstone Castle has battlements and looks like a castle but the present appearance dates only from the beginning of the nineteenth century. There were originally two manors here, Chiddingstone Cobham and Chiddingstone Burgherst. The former was held in 1341 by Reginald de Cobham, a member of this famous Kentish family. It came into the hands of the Burgh family but, when this line died out in 1598, it was sold to the Streatfeilds who were to be associated with Chiddingstone until 1936. The other manor was owned by a famous Sussex family, the first holder being Reynold Burgherst in the thirteenth century. His son, Robert, was a constable of Dover Castle and Lord Warden of the Cinque Ports and was granted a barony. His grandson, Bartholomew, was a distinguished soldier who fought in the French wars of Edward III. He was only a boy when he took part in the Battle of Crécy and was in the Black Prince's army at Poitiers. This manor then passed through several hands before being sold to the Streatfeilds in 1700 and so this family thus owned both the Chiddingstone properties.

The Streatfeilds are first recorded at Chiddingstone in 1514. They never seemed to be ambitious to become national figures but were content to live quietly in their country home, looking after the property and their tenants and enlarging the estate so that by the end of the nineteenth century they owned nearly 8,000 acres in the county of Kent. They steadfastly refused to stand for Parliament and their only concession to high office was to serve occasionally as a High Sheriff of Kent.

Henry Streatfeild was responsible for demolishing the old property and building himself a red-brick mansion with fine gardens and terraces in 1789. His great-grandson, a hundred years later, refaced the building in sandstone, and added towers, turrets and battlements so that it looked like a castle. The village High Street was diverted to make room for a lake of three acres.

Further improvements were made by his son a few years later when more towers and long windows were added. Pine and oak panelling was put into the interior and a stable block and a covered way from the kitchen constructed.

When Col. Sir Henry Streatfeild, who had been Queen Alexandra's private secretary, died in 1936 the castle became a school. During the war the army moved in and the late Field-Marshal Viscount Montgomery held a number of parades there before he went out to Egypt to command the Eighth Army. Anti-aircraft guns were mounted in the park and, for the first time, Chiddingstone played the part of a real castle with a garrison of 300 soldiers.

In 1955 Chiddingstone was sold to Mr Denys Eyre Bower who stocked it with his collections from all parts of the world and opened it to the public. In addition to exhibits from India, Tibet, China, Egypt and Japan, there are some splendid relics of the Stuart kings.

Here is Lely's nude portrait of Nell Gwynne, painted for Charles II, and a silver heart-shaped reliquary containing part of the heart of James II which was brought to this country at the time of the French Revolution. There is a fine collection of letters and documents from Mary Queen of Scots, James I, Charles I, Charles II and James II and the last letter pleading for his life written by the Duke of Monmouth (illegitimate son of Charles II) to his uncle James II. The famous letter written by Bonnie Prince Charlie to his father before setting out for Scotland and the '45 Rising is shown together with locks of hair of Mary Queen of Scots, Charles I, Charles II and James II. There is also the drinking cup used by Bonnie Prince Charlie in the Highlands.

Much older than any of these is another drinking cup used by an Egyptian princess. This dates from 1000 B.C. This collection alone makes Chiddingstone a worthy neighbour of the two other historic houses, Penshurst and Hever, which stand within a few miles of it.

Penshurst Place, the house of the Sidneys, is without doubt one of the great showplaces of this country. Many thousands of visitors come here every year and it is no wonder for this is the finest example of a medieval mansion in the country.

Domesday Book of 1085 mentions an important house at

Penshurst but the first recorded owner is Sir Stephen de Penchester in the thirteenth century. He was also a constable of Dover Castle and Lord Warden of the Cinque Ports. In 1338 Penshurst was in possession of a lord mayor of London, Sir John de Pulteney, who built the magnificent Great Hall which can still be seen. He died in the Black Death and a later owner was the Duke of Buckingham who entertained Henry VIII to a splendid feast in the Great Hall. This brought him little good for, shortly afterwards, he fell out of favour, was beheaded, and the king seized Penshurst.

It remained a royal estate until Edward VI presented it to his chamberlain and steward, Sir William Sidney, in 1552. This started the Sidney ownership of Penshurst which has continued to this day. Sir William had fought with the English army against the Scots at Flodden and accompanied Henry VIII on his visit to France and the famous 'Field of the Cloth of Gold'. He was to enjoy Penshurst for only two years before he died and was succeeded by his son, Henry. This Sidney, however, saw little of his estate for he was employed constantly by Queen Elizabeth and spent long periods in Ireland and Wales. His wife was Lady May Dudley, daughter of the Duke of Northumberland, who was beheaded when he attempted to place his daughter-in-law, Lady Jane Grey, on the throne.

Sir Henry, who was a boyhood friend of Edward VI, prudently decided not to back his father-in-law's scheme and so continued in royal favour during Queen Mary's reign. He spent much of this period in Ireland as vice-treasurer of the Irish Court. In Elizabeth's reign he became President of Wales and lived at Ludlow Castle, although as his duties were nominal, he contrived to spend much time at court. When Irish affairs worsened in 1566 he went back there to attempt to put down the rebellion. He was responsible for the erection of the first bridge over the River Shannon, having had to swim across the river on one of his journeys. He had Dublin Castle rebuilt but his rule proved to be too expensive for Elizabeth who recalled him in 1578. He resumed his duties in Wales but, worn out and ill, he died in 1586. By the queen's command his body was brought home for burial at Penshurst.

His eldest son was the famous Sir Philip Sidney, the

soldier, courtier and poet who is best known in history for his death. Badly wounded at the Battle of Zutphen and parched with thirst, he handed over his water bottle to a wounded foot soldier with the words, "Thy need is greater than mine".

Philip was named after his godfather, Philip II of Spain, the husband of Queen Mary. He spent his boyhood at Penshurst where he 'quickly established himself as a scholar. By the age of eleven he was writing letters and poems in English and Latin. As a youth, he soon came to the notice of the queen's secretary, Sir William Cecil, who introduced him to the court. He was given the queen's licence to spend two years on the Continent to study languages and was attached to the embassy in Paris. He also visited Germany and Vienna and spent some time in Venice where he was befriended by the painter Tintoretto and studied music, literature, history and astronomy. Later he went on to Poland and to Germany and Holland before returning home.

At Penshurst he superintended, on behalf of his absent father, improvements to the house and estate. His life at court seems to have come under a cloud and this was exacerbated when he published a paper condemning the queen's proposed marriage to the Duke of Anjou. He made amends by presenting the queen with a gold-headed whip, a gold chain and a heart of gold in 1581.

When an army was sent to the Low Countries in 1585 to fight the Spanish, Philip, although anxious to join the fleet of Sir Francis Drake, was appointed to command the garrison at Flushing. An attack upon the Spanish stronghold at Zutphen was ordered. Philip's horse was killed under him, but mounting another he charged at the enemy troops. He was hit by a bullet in the leg but managed to remain on his horse until he reached the English camp. The wound failed to heal and he died on 17 October 1586. His funeral was at St Paul's Cathedral and was attended by 700 mourners. The tomb was destroyed in the Great Fire of London in 1666.

A younger brother, Robert, succeeded to the ownership of Penshurst, to be raised by James I to Viscount Lisle and then Earl of Leicester. He spent all his leisure time at Penshurst where he added the long gallery on to the existing building. A great friend of James I, he entertained the king on hunting expeditions at the estate. Another Robert, his son, succeeded

him and was employed by Charles I on missions abroad.
When the Civil War broke out he quietly retired to
Penshurst and took no part in the fighting, but his sons,
Philip and Algernon, actively supported the Parliamentarians. Philip was a member of the Council of State and one
of the judges at the trial of Charles I, although he withdrew
from this position. When Oliver Cromwell died he signed the
proclamation declaring his son, Richard Cromwell, the new
Protector. On the return of Charles II he managed to obtain
a pardon.

The other son, Algernon, fought as a cavalry commander
with the parliamentary army and was wounded at Marston
Moor. Appointed one of the commissioners for the king's
trial, he then refused to act as a judge as he maintained that
the king could not be tried by a court. By this action he
incurred the enmity of Cromwell and took little part in
public affairs for the next three years. He came to regard
Cromwell as a tyrant and had a play performed at
Penshurst, in which he played the leading role, which was
described as an insult to the Lord Protector. At the Restoration he was abroad and in danger of arrest as a regicide.
Settling in Germany, he did not return to England for
another seventeen years but was arrested in 1683 in connection with the Rye House Plot to murder the king.
Evidence against him would appear to have been in-
conclusive but he was browbeaten by the notorious Judge
Jeffreys and sentenced to death. He sent a petition to the
king protesting at the illegality of the trial but was beheaded
on Tower Hill on 7 December 1683.

The youngest brother, Henry, was also active in politics
and was intriguing against the new king James II. He was
one of the six who signed the letter inviting William of
Orange to come over and seize the throne. Henry sailed with
William to the landing at Brixham and later fought with his
army at the Battle of the Boyne.

In 1835 Philip Shelley, who had descended through the
female line, was created Lord de Lisle and Dudley and set to
work to repair and renovate the house and estate which had
suffered during the years of neglect. The present owner
succeeded to the title as the fifth Lord de Lisle in 1945.
Fighting in Italy during the Second World War, he won the

Victoria Cross at the battle which followed the Anzio landing. He was Secretary of State for Air from 1951 to 1955 and Governor-General of Australia from 1961 to 1965.

The work of preserving and restoring Penshurst continues and visitors can still see the Great Hall which dates back to the fourteenth century. The chestnut beamed timber roof is 60 feet high with ten life-sized figures which look down from above. Here are the trestle tables which were used when Edward IV dined at Penshurst. They were also used for the banquet given for Henry VIII by the Duke of Buckingham. Here also is Sir Philip Sidney's helmet which was carried in his funeral procession to St Paul's.

Armour and weapons of all periods are on display in the crypt and also the state sword presented to Field-Marshal Viscount Gort V.C. by the people of Malta after the siege in the Second World War. In the long gallery is the leaden death mask of Queen Elizabeth and portraits of most of the Sidney ancestors.

The gardens and orchards reflect the Tudor atmosphere of Penshurst. These have always been noteworthy and were remarked upon by John Evelyn, the diarist, when he visited Penshurst in 1652 as "famous for its gardens and excellent fruit". Lily ponds are stocked with goldfish and a feature of these gardens is the number and variety of sundials.

Penshurst has survived remarkably well its 900 years as a great house and estate. It stands quietly and proudly aware of its great history and of being the home of the great Sidney family for the last 400 years.

The picturesque moated castle of Hever was the home of Anne Boleyn, the ill-fated second queen of Henry VIII. Following years of neglect it has been carefully restored to its former self and is a fine example of one of the few inhabited medieval castles in the country.

Hever was built as a manor house by Thomas de Hever in the reign of Edward III. It was then a farm building with a yard surrounded by a moat with a wooden drawbridge. In 1462 it was bought by Sir Geoffrey de Boleyn who pulled down the old building and replaced it with a castle, having received permission to crenellate or fortify the building. His grandson, Sir Thomas Boleyn, inherited the place in 1506 and he was the father of Anne Boleyn. It was at Hever that Henry VIII first met Anne and it was here that he courted her.

Anne was born in 1507, the youngest daughter of Sir Thomas. She spent her early years in France, having gone there in the suite of Mary, the sister of Henry VIII, who married Louis XII. She was to stay there for seven years as one of the French queen's attendants and did not come home until 1522 when she was fifteen. A lively, beautiful girl with sparkling black eyes, she soon had plenty of admirers, including Sir Thomas Wyatt of Allington Castle. Lord Henry Percy, heir to the Earl of Northumberland, proposed marriage but was warned off by Cardinal Wolsey, acting on the king's instructions.

Henry was certainly interested in her but she resisted all his advances until he offered to make her his queen as soon as he could get rid of his wife, Katherine of Aragon. He instructed Wolsey to obtain a divorce but the Pope, a captive of Katherine's Spanish nephew, refused to have anything to do with it. Henry settled the problem by divorcing England from the Church of Rome and then getting his own divorce from the newly created Church of England.

Anne had already been installed in magnificent apartments at Greenwich. Although members of the court accepted her, she was hated and reviled by the crowds in the street. She and the king were married on 25 January 1533 and later she was crowned at a magnificent ceremony in Westminster Hall.

Her daughter, the future Queen Elizabeth, was born in the September but this was a great disappointment to the king who wanted a son and heir. Henry soon tired of her and started gathering evidence of her alleged adultery so that he could be rid of her to marry Jane Seymour. In 1536 he was ready. Anne was arrested and sent to the Tower of London, charged with adultery with her brother, three courtiers and her musician. She was brought to trial before a panel of twenty-six peers presided over by her uncle, the Duke of Norfolk. All the peers, including her father, voted her guilty and she was sentenced to death by burning or beheading. Four days later an executioner from Calais beheaded her with a sword.

Not surprisingly, her ghost is said to haunt Hever Castle, but she only appears, gliding over the bridge, once a year on Christmas Eve. A strange choice, for it was not the day of her birth, nor that of her marriage nor of her execution.

Her father, Sir Thomas, who had been created Earl of Wiltshire, did not long survive and Henry gave the castle to his divorced fourth wife, Anne of Cleves, and she kept it for seventeen years. It then passed through the hands of many owners but was being more and more neglected until it was rescued in 1903. William Waldorf Astor, an American who came to this country and became a British subject, fell in love with Hever, bought it and decided to restore it.

This was a mammoth task for which 2,000 men were employed. A complete village in the Tudor style was built to provide guest rooms, servants' quarters and offices of the estate, all connected by corridors and to the castle by a covered bridge across the moat. A 35-acre lake was dug out from the rank marsh and fed by the River Eden. Hundreds of tons of soil and rock were moved to provide the ground for the large selection of trees and shrubs which were imported. In the gardens were constructed paved courtyards, rose gardens, orchards, a maze and a yew hedge cut as a set of chessmen.

Overlooking the lake is a colonnaded piazza with Italian gardens, fountains, grottoes and cascades. Into these were placed the classic marble statues which Mr Astor had collected when he was the American Minister in Rome. All these improvements which rescued the old castle from neglect and decay cost huge sums of money. It was an act of great faith on the part of Mr Astor to undertake such a vast operation and, as Hever is open to the public, his work can be enjoyed by all.

The castle itself is also full of treasures. There are many fine paintings by Holbein, Titian and others. In the Henry VIII room is the bed which belonged to Anne Boleyn and a mirror which belonged to her daughter, Queen Elizabeth. A torture chamber contains a collection of instruments of torture used in the Middle Ages.

The tower of Hadlow Castle can be seen for many miles and this is given as one of the reasons why it was built. It is not a castle at all but a folly erected in 1840 by Walter Barton May. There are many of these follies to be found in the county, some being sham castles, others 'ruined' monasteries, towers, gatehouses, arches, obelisks, grottoes and 'Stonehenges'. They were built by wealthy landowners for a variety of reasons—to add something to the landscape, to create a romantic medieval atmosphere or just to satisfy a whim.

The reason for May's Folly is unknown. He had previously built sham battlements on to the mansion below and it was said that he wanted to build vertically. In this he succeeded for his tower soars to a height of 170 feet. Another explanation is that his wife had deserted him and gone to live elsewhere in Kent. He put up his tower so that she would see it and be reminded of him wherever she was. A third reason is given that he had been told that if he was buried in the earth his family would lose all its possessions and so he planned that his coffin should rest at the top of the tower. If this is correct his wishes were ignored for his body lies in a handsome mausoleum in Hadlow church.

The tower was constructed between 1838 and 1840 by George Taylor, architect and engineer to the Royal Navy. It is octagonal with gabled projections. The castellated mansion has gone but the slim Gothic brick-built tower remains. If it is a monument to one man's folly it is, at least, pleasant to look at and certainly no eye-sore.

A few miles further along the road to Maidstone is Mereworth Castle. This, again, is not a castle but a splendid Palladian villa. Mereworth is now in private hands but can be seen from the road.

It was built at a cost of £100,000 for the Earl of Westmoreland between 1720 and 1748 and to make way for it the village and the church were demolished and built again a mile to the west. The building was designed by Colin Campbell in imitation of Palladio's famous villa which overlooks Vicenza. Mereworth is larger than the original for it is a 90-foot square with a dome of 38 feet in diameter over its 55 foot high roof. The decorations were equally splendid with the painted ceiling of the dome bearing classical motifs. A balustraded gallery runs round the upper part of the walls.

Mereworth is certainly beautiful but one does not know the feelings of the vicar and the villagers who were unceremoniously uprooted and dumped down further along the road.

The church which was built in 1744 is certainly impressive with Doric columns and a steeple which was copied from St Martin-in-the-Fields in Trafalgar Square. As the previous church could not have looked so grand and imposing, one can only suppose that the parishioners were satisfied.

5

Maidstone and the Medway Valley

MAIDSTONE is the county town and the centre of the brewing industry. Hops are traditionally associated with Kent and the conical oast houses are a familiar sight.

Formerly the hops were picked by hand and every autumn hordes of Londoners would come into the county by special trains for the 'hopping'. This was their annual holiday and an industrious family could make it a profitable one. The villagers greeted this invasion with mixed feelings for although the publicans and shopkeepers did good business, the Londoners were notorious for stealing from orchards and for fighting with the police and populace. In modern times the picking of hops is done by machines and this casual labour is not required.

Penenden Heath, on the outskirts of the town, was a traditional meeting place for the county for many years. The Saxons held their moots here and it was the scene of one of the first recorded trials when Archbishop Lanfranc brought an action against Odo, Earl of Kent, for the recovery of some of his estates.

The archbishops held a palace at Maidstone and it is still there in almost its original state. It is now used by the local Corporation. Near here is All Saints' Church, much visited by Americans for it has the tomb of Lawrence Washington, an ancestor of George Washington. His arms, above the tomb, bear the stars and stripes which were later to form the flag of the United States.

The town is now the possessor of the magnificent Mote Park which was bought by the Corporation in 1929. It was in the ownership of Roger de Leybourne in 1265 and later came into the possession of the Woodville family. Kent then had the honour of providing another queen of England when Elizabeth Woodville married Edward IV. Her father, Richard, held the estate which, on his death, passed to her brother Anthony, Lord Rivers. He lived in a mansion above the lake and was renowned as a patron of the arts. Caxton was given active encouragement by him to produce fine books and Mote Park was recognized as having a fine collection of manuscripts and works of art.

The Woodville family prospered during the reign of Edward IV but, after his death, it was discovered that it was a bigamous marriage and the children by it were declared illegitimate. The new king, Richard III, had no love for the Woodvilles whom he suspected of plotting against him. Anthony Woodville was executed and Mote Park was seized and given to Sir Robert Brackenbury, Lieutenant of the Tower of London. Brackenbury was killed at the Battle of Bosworth and Henry VII gave Mote Park back to the Woodvilles.

For a time it was in the possession of the Wyatt family but they lost it when Thomas Wyatt staged the rebellion against Queen Mary. It later went to Sir John Marsham who was created Earl of Romney. He pulled down the old house and erected a new building on the other side of the lake in 1799. He completed it just in time to entertain George III who, with Queen Charlotte, the Prince of Wales, the Dukes of Cumberland and Gloucester and the Princesses Augusta and Elizabeth, attended a grand review of the Kentish volunteers pledged to repel Napoleon. This took place in the valley where the old house stood and where there is now a stone pavilion erected in Lord Romney's honour by the volunteers. After the march past there was a mock battle and then the whole company of 6,000 sat down to a banquet provided by the earl. The tables to accommodate this company stretched for $7\frac{1}{2}$ miles. The king made a speech in which he praised the martial spirit of the volunteers who then formed a guard of honour for the departure of the royal family.

Mote Park passed through several hands before becoming a public park. The mansion is now a Cheshire Home.

The River Len which feeds the lake in Mote Park also provides the moat which surrounds Leeds Castle, a few miles away on the road to Ashford. This is everyone's idea of what a medieval castle should be. Its towers and battlements are reflected in the water and, apart from the provision of windows and electricity, can be seen today much as it was when it was held as a strong fortress. It looks so perfect that one wonders if it is real but it has, of course, been carefully restored in the last century. This has been done so well that only the most pedantic architect would complain. But for the vast sums of money spent on its restoration it would undoubtedly have decayed and become ruinous as have so many other castles in the county.

A castle or fort was first built here in 857 by a Saxon chief named Led. After the Norman Conquest, Hugh de Crevecour built the stone keep. He was one of the captains of Dover Castle and held other lands in Kent. A descendant, Robert de Crevecour, joined the forces of Simon de Montfort in the war against Henry III and forfeited the castle and the estate which went to his supporters, the Leybourne family. When Robert de Leybourne died while fighting in the crusades the castle passed into royal hands and Edward I presented it to his queen, Eleanor of Castille, who greatly enlarged and improved it. The next queen, Isabella of France, allowed it to be occupied by the Kentish knight Bartholomew de Badlesmere who appointed Walter Culpepper of Hollingbourne as its captain. Bartholomew then went off to join the rebellion against Edward II and while he was away Queen Isabella arrived with a large retinue and demanded admittance. Lady Badlesmere, who was in the castle with her children, feared that the queen wanted to seize it for her husband and instructed Culpepper to keep her out. Furious at this insult, Queen Isabella complained to the king and Edward promptly moved against Leeds with an army of 30,000 men. Leeds was besieged and eventually obliged to surrender. Culpepper and the garrison were executed and Lady Badlesmere and the children sent to imprisonment in the Tower of London. Bartholomew was later captured and beheaded at Canterbury.

Leeds continued to be a royal castle and both Edward II and Richard II were constant visitors and carried out improvements. Many jousting tournaments were held in the park, especially in the reign of Henry VIII who regarded himself as a master of this art.

Edward VI gave Leeds to the St Leger family but they lost their money when they invested in Sir Walter Raleigh's expedition to Guiana and were forced to sell the castle and the park. It then passed into the hands of the Culpeppers, descendants of the unfortunate Walter who had defied Queen Isabella. Siding with the royalists in the Civil War, they forfeited the castle but it was returned to them by Charles II. Fortunately it had escaped the slighting which many castles suffered whose owners had supported the king.

For a time Leeds was used as a prison for the French and Dutch prisoners-of-war and John Evelyn was appointed commissioner and charged with looking after their interests. He was often at Leeds during this period.

It had previously been used as a prison for Richard II and for Eleanor of Gloucester, the aunt of Henry VI, who was found guilty of "necromancy, witchcraft, heresy and treason".

In the nineteenth century the owner Wykeham Martin restored and repaired the castle and it is to him that credit must be given for the preservation of this magnificent building described by another lover of castles, Lord Conway, as "the loveliest castle in the whole world".

The last private owner was Lady Olive Baillie and on her death Leeds was presented to a charitable trust and is open to the public during the summer. The castle stands on two islands in the middle of a lake. The first is reached through a massive gatehouse with arrow-slits and machiolated turrets. The main keep or gloriette was built by Edward I but an upper storey was added in Tudor times. The splendid park was laid out by Capability Brown.

Leeds is worth going miles to see and many visitors now come to the castle which previously they had seen only through the trees on the main road. Standards fly from the towers and it needs little imagination to see knights cantering out over the drawbridge with fair damsels waving their kerchiefs from the battlements. Forget the electric light and glass panes in the windows and enjoy Leeds as a medieval castle which has come straight out of the picture books.

A few miles to the north-east of Leeds once stood one of the most famous abbeys in the land. Just off the Pilgrims' Way, along which the pilgrims made their journey to Canterbury, was Boxley Abbey. Such was its fame that pilgrims turned aside and visited it for the miracles which were performed there. These miracles brought the house into disrepute when finally exposed as frauds when the abbey was dissolved by Henry VIII.

Kent was liberally endowed with monasteries and nunneries in the Middle Ages and nearly every religious order was represented. There were six Benedictine monasteries and six Benedictine nunneries. The Austin Canons held six houses, the Premonstratensians two, the Franciscans three and the Carmelite friars two. The county also had single houses of Cluniac monks, Cistercian monks, Dominican friars, Dominican nuns and Austin friars in addition to four establishments of the military religious orders, the Knights Templar and Knights Hospitaller. All these religious orders could be traced back to St Benedict who laid down simple and strict rules of monastic life. As time went on new monastic orders were founded which differed from those of the Benedictines. The harshest was that of the Cistercians whose rules specified that the monastery must not be built in a town but in a wild place away from worldly affairs where they would have to fend for themselves. Their main areas were in the vast expanses of wild and uncultivated land in the north. The Cluniacs, on the other hand, devoted all their time to church services and employed servants to carry out the work in the gardens and fields. The Carthusians aimed at a life of simple piety. Each monk lived in a little cell in almost complete solitude and obeyed the vow of silence. The friars, however, went out preaching to the people and built large churches to which they invited the local population.

Monasteries and nunneries varied in size. Each was ruled by an abbot or abbess and was, for the most part, self-contained. A strict adherence to the rules of the order meant a harsh life devoted to service to God. There were eight services each day in the church, starting with one at 2.00 a.m. with another two before dawn. The last service of the day, compline, would not be until 8.00 p.m. In between the services the monks worked in the fields, prepared meals, studied or painted. Meals varied from the bread with two vegetables in the Cistercian houses to the poultry, venison, fish and wine provided in the Benedictine houses. The monastery served not only as a centre of religion but as a hospital, library, school and farm for the local community.

In the latter years of the monasteries it is quite clear that the monks and nuns were paying only lip-service to the rules of their various orders. There are numerous cases reported by bishops in their visitations to the religious houses that a sorry state of affairs existed. Monks were to be found in the taverns of the nearest town, women were entertained in the monasteries, services were skipped, nights were spent in drinking parties and gaming and gambling openly indulged in. Although Henry VIII and his minister, Thomas Cromwell, have been condemned for seizing the monasteries and turning out the monks, it would seem that, certainly in the south, there was some justification for the charges made against the religious orders. The monks preyed upon the gullible visitors to extract alms and many monasteries amassed a great deal of wealth.

Boxley Abbey was exposed as being one of the worst offenders in this respect. It was a Cistercian abbey, the only one in Kent, founded by William de Ypres in 1146 as a penance for his sins. He had a bad reputation as a local tyrant until he became blind and turned to religion in the hope of a cure. Boxley owed its fame to two holy relics which the monks claimed could perform miracles. One of these was a small stone figure of St Rumbold. Those who were chaste and pure in heart could easily lift this statue but for others it stayed rooted to the ground. The monks would suggest that prayer and the gift of alms might make the pilgrim chaste and pure and this would be the case, as the figure could then be lifted. When the abbey was dissolved the trick was discovered. The figure was held in place by a hidden device. When sufficient alms had been donated to the abbey, a monk, standing behind the statue, would release a catch and it could then be lifted.

The other relic was the Rood of Grace. This was a figure which could bow its head, nod, roll its eyes, smile or frown. It was made by a carpenter who had been taken prisoner-of-war in France and constructed it out of wood, wire, paste and paper to pass the time. Upon his release the carpenter brought the figure back to England. On a journey to Rochester he went into a house leaving the figure strapped to the back of his horse. The horse wandered away and came to Boxley Abbey. When the carpenter eventually arrived the monks had discovered the mechanism of the figure. The carpenter was forced to sell it to them for a small sum of money and the figure was then set up in the church.

The Rood was a great attraction to the pilgrims. It would answer questions by a nod or a shake of the head, smile upon them for good fortune or frown if displeased. Its attitude, of course, depended upon the amount of alms offered up by the pilgrim. A frown would greet a small donation but this could be altered to a smile by increasing the gift.

At the dissolution of Boxley Abbey in 1538 the Rood was publicly exhibited in Maidstone and then burnt on the steps of St Paul's in London after a sermon condemning it had been delivered by the Bishop of Rochester. The Rood was operated by a monk from the back who pulled levers and wires to give the right effect. It was found to contain "certain engines of old wyer, with old rotten sticks in the back" which "caused the eyes to move and stir – the head like unto a live thing and also the nether lip to move as though it should speak".

When tackled about this fraud the abbot and monks professed ignorance and maintained that the figure was operated by a miracle. Lambarde is typically scathing on the matter which he called "a notable imposture, fraud, jugglery and legerdemain by which the sillie lambes of God's flock were not long since seduced by the false Romish foxes at the Abbey. These monks, to their own enriching and the spoile of God's people, abused this wooden God". Lambarde says that if he failed to report these frauds "the favourers of false and feigned religion would laugh in their sleeves and the followers of God's truth might justly cry out and blame me".

The abbot was pensioned off with £50 a year – a sizable sum in those days – and the abbey and lands given to the Wyatt family at Allington Castle. Years of neglect and decay have taken their toll. There is now only the great tithe barn, some ivy-covered walls and the arch of the gatehouse to be seen. This once-great religious house, a centre of learning and of community life, is now only remembered for the frauds perpetrated upon the unsuspecting pilgrims in the guise of miracles. These frauds provided welcome ammunition for Henry and Thomas Cromwell when they set out to justify the dissolution of the monasteries by showing up the corrupt practices which were then employed.

Allington Castle, a few miles down the River Medway from Maidstone, is another fine romantic castle which, like Leeds, has been carefully repaired and restored. It is beautifully situated at a bend in the river and is widely accepted as one of the most splendid examples of a medieval castle in the country.

Standing on the site of a Roman camp, Allington was first of all a Saxon manor owned by Wulfnorth, fourth son of Earl Godwin and brother of King Harold. After the Norman Conquest it went to the Conqueror's half-brother, Odo, Earl of Kent, and then, following his disgrace, to William de Warenne who built a castle. It passed to William de Allington, probably his son, who extended, improved and strengthened it during the civil wars in the reign of King Stephen. This William was also known as William de Colombes from the many doves which he kept on the estate. Two of his dovecots, believed to be the oldest in the country, are still there today.

When Henry II came to the throne he classified Allington as an adulterine castle which had been erected without royal licence and ordered it to be destroyed. This was done by the sheriff at a cost of 6 shillings. The de Colombes, deprived of their castle, built a manor house in its place. In 1281 it was bought by Sir Stephen de Penchester (whom we met at Penshurst Place). He applied for and was granted a licence to crenellate (to fortify) and built the castle, some parts of which we can still see today. A great hall was erected, the machiolated gatehouse built up and strengthened and towers were constructed along the curtain wall.

In 1492 Allington Castle was purchased by the Wyatt family and entered into history with the stormy careers of its owners. Sir Henry Wyatt, a fervent Lancastrian, was bitterly opposed to Richard III when he seized the throne in 1482 after declaring his brother's marriage invalid and his sons, 'the princes in the Tower', illegitimate. Wyatt was arrested and spent two years in the Tower of London where, according to his family, he was put on the rack in the presence of the king.

There is a legend that Sir Henry, while in the Tower, was saved from starvation by a friendly cat. Every day this cat came to the window of his cell with a pigeon which it had taken from a neighbouring dovecot. On this diet of pigeons, cooked by a friendly gaoler, Sir Henry managed to survive until the Battle of Bosworth brought about the death of Richard III and the accession of Henry VII. He was promptly released and went back to Allington Castle where it is recorded that "he would ever make much of cats as other men will of their spaniels and hounds".

The star of the Wyatt family was now in the ascendant. Sir Henry was appointed a guardian of the young Prince Henry (afterwards Henry VIII) and treasurer to the king. When he died in 1537 he was succeeded by his only son, the poet Sir Thomas. This young man was widely regarded as the lover of Anne Boleyn of Hever Castle although he had himself married Elizabeth, daughter of Lord Cobham, when he was only seventeen. This was to cause him some trouble and danger when Henry VIII courted and married Anne.

Sir Thomas travelled abroad frequently on the king's business. While returning from a visit to Venice he was captured by the imperial forces and a ransom of 3,000 ducats was demanded, but Wyatt contrived to escape during the night and reached Bologna. He was still in favour at court and was created high-marshal of Calais. At Anne Boleyn's coronation in 1533 he acted as chief ewerer and poured scented water over the queen's hands.

When Henry found out about Anne's adultery, Wyatt was in trouble. He was arrested and thrown into the Tower but found an unexpected friend in Thomas Cromwell who contrived his release. Presumably no evidence was produced against him for the Wyatt family continued in royal favour and his sister, Mary, attended Anne Boleyn on the scaffold. Cromwell, now a powerful minister, treated him well and Sir Thomas was appointed ambassador to the court of Spain.

In the course of his diplomatic career, Wyatt had made enemies and complaints were made to Cromwell that he was engaged in treasonable activities and was leading a disgraceful life. Cromwell, a stalwart friend of Wyatt, ignored these accusations, but when he too fell foul of Henry VIII and was executed in 1541, the charges were renewed. Wyatt went to the Tower again but was soon released back into royal favour and given the estate of Boxley Abbey which had recently been suppressed. He lived for only one more year and died at the age of thirty-nine.

Wyatt acquired a high reputation as a poet and is regarded as the man who introduced the sonnet from Italy into this country. His poems were first printed in 1557 and have been reprinted since.

Another Thomas, the eldest surviving son, now held Allington Castle. He also married young but was known to be a wild and impulsive youth. He saw the inside of the Tower of London at the age of twenty-two when he and some others were arrested after an escapade in London. They stormed through the city, breaking windows in houses and churches and, when brought before the privy council, were charged not only with these offences, but with having eaten meat during Lent.

Wyatt spent four weeks as a prisoner but then joined a regiment of volunteers for the fighting on the continent. He played a distinguished part at the sieges of Landrecies and Boulogne until ill-health forced him to come home.

When Queen Mary announced her intention of marrying Philip II of Spain there was an outcry from some parts of the country. Wyatt undertook to raise an army in Kent to fight what he described as "an outrage to the nation's honour". On 22 January 1554 he called a meeting of friends and neighbours at Allington Castle and plans for the campaign were drawn up. They went to Maidstone where a proclamation was published calling for volunteers to fight for the advancement of liberty and commonwealth "which are imperilled by the queen's determinate pleasure to marry with a stranger".

Wyatt soon had an army of 1,500 men and they marched to Rochester Castle which he made his headquarters. Cannon and ammunition had been sent in by secret agents in London and the guns were sited to command Rochester bridge and the opposite side of the river. He kept up the spirits of his army by circulating false reports of other risings in all parts of the country and by the promise of the support of French troops.

Queen Mary, who quickly promised pardons to all who would desert Wyatt, sent out a force to put down the rebellion. The Duke of Norfolk, at the head of about 1,000 men, set off, but when they came to Rochester many of them left and went over to Wyatt's army. The duke and his staff fled rapidly back to Gravesend.

Wyatt then set out for London at the head of 4,000 men. He had already been proclaimed a traitor and knew the fate which awaited him if he should fail. The queen enrolled an army of 20,000 men to protect the city of London, had the bridges over the Thames destroyed and offered a reward of land to the value of £100 a year to anyone who captured Wyatt.

The rebel army marched into Southwark but were compelled by the guns from the Tower of London to withdraw. Wyatt then decided to move up the river, cross it at Kingston and capture London from the west. He succeeded in this to the extent that he and his army crossed the river, came through Kensington and routed a troop of infantry in a skirmish at Hyde Park Corner. They moved on to the city but all the gates were firmly shut. His followers had now started to desert and Wyatt was forced to surrender. He was found guilty of high treason and sentenced to the terrible death which awaited traitors.

The Wyatt family later left England for America. They settled in Virginia and their descendants are welcome visitors to Allington Castle when they come over to see their ancestral home.

Allington Castle was sequestered by the queen and given to the Astley family of Maidstone. Little was done to keep it in repair and it deteriorated rapidly. At one stage it was being used as a prison. A fire seriously damaged the great hall, the chapel and one of the towers. It was not until 1905 that serious repair work was done by a lover of castles, Lord Conway, who spent the next twenty-five years in restoring it at the cost of £25,000.

Martin Conway, son of the vicar of St Nicholas, Rochester, was a man of many parts. He was a Member of Parliament, mountaineer, antiquarian and, above all, interested in medieval castles. In 1905 he inserted an advertisement in a newspaper: "Wanted to purchase, an old manor house or abbey built in the 16th century or earlier." One of the replies offered Allington Castle for sale. He and his wife drove down to see it. Writing later, he described their reactions to the first sight of the ruined castle "Everywhere roses were in full bloom. They rampaged over the ruins and formed high hedges where inner walls had been. The beauty of it all was entrancing. It took our breath away and for a moment we were speechless. Then we both gasped out – of course we must have it."

The freehold was purchased for a sum of only £4,800 and Lord Conway was faced with the daunting task of restoration, repair and rebuilding.

The old castle, which had been slowly slipping away, was restored to health. Its ancient battlements were repaired, towers and turrets restored to the original condition and the interior converted into a comfortable home. All this was done with care so that what is now seen is a typical medieval castle and not a fanciful Walt Disney-type creation. Many castles have been suffered to fall into decay without finding a fairy godfather to rescue them, but in recent years the Department of the Environment has done wonderful work in looking after those committed to its care.

Following a period in the ownership of Sir Alfred Bossom, then M.P. for Maidstone, Allington Castle was bought for £15,000 by the Carmelite Order as a centre for ecumenical and youth work. It is regularly open to the public.

The entrance is through the massive gatehouse which still has the grooves for the portcullis. Solomon's Tower, the old keep in the inner courtyard, is named after a Solomon de Allington who was the local lord of the manor back in the twelfth century. Beyond is a lovely garden which was used in the old days as a tiltyard where tournaments were held.

The old castle is now a living entity, rescued in the nick of time when it was slipping into complete ruin.

Although the Ordnance Survey maps show a castle at Thurnham, a village on the Pilgrim's Way below the North Downs, it is difficult to find. Up the steep hill and off a turning in the thick undergrowth are the few pathetic remains of castle walls. The site is magnificent for it has natural protection on three sides by the steep slope of the downs and a view for a very long way to the south.

There was a Roman watchtower on this site before the castle was built by a Saxon named Godard. It is mentioned as Godard's Castle in the charter of 1215 when the owner, Robert de Thurnham, was away fighting in the crusades. He apparently did not return, the family and the servants left and the castle was allowed to decay.

Thurnham, however, had a better claim to fame in the history of Kent. In the churchyard at the foot of the hill is the grave of Alfred Mynn, the 'Lion of Kent' as he was named in his prime. Mynn was a cricketer in the early part of the nineteenth century and was rightly regarded as the greatest match winner of all time.

Mynn was champion of England at single wicket for many years and was one of the first of the round-arm bowlers, having been taught by John Willes of Sutton Valence. Willes himself had picked up this style of bowling from his sister Christine, who was a keen cricketer and used to practise with him. Wearing the crinolines of those days she could not bowl in the recognized underarm style and so raised her arm to the shoulder and bowled round-arm. She was a deadly bowler and it was said at the time that John Willes, Christine and his dog (a fox terrier which fielded the ball with its mouth) could beat any team in England. Willes saw the possibilities, practised in this style and coached Alfred Mynn in it.

Born at Goudhurst, Mynn played much of his early cricket for the village team at Leeds. He was soon recognized as a leading cricketer of the day and picked for the England teams. His career nearly came to a sad and premature end when he was injured playing for the South against the North at Leicester in 1836. He was hit on the ankle which swelled up and made even walking painful. In spite of this he bowled and then scored 125 not out from a total of 223. He was unable to climb into the stage coach for the return journey and so he was strapped on top. When he got to London he was told the leg would have to be amputated but he protested so vigorously that the doctors agreed to wait and see if there would be an improvement. Mynn recovered and was playing cricket in the next season.

He was a popular character wherever he went and, in those days of bribery, was essentially honest. Approached by a baronet with a bribe to sell a match, he threatened to knock him down. On his death he was commemorated in a poem as "kind and manly Alfred Mynn" and a memorial fund was started to make grants to deserving Kent cricketers. This fund still exists today, more than 100 years after his death, administered by the Kent County Cricket Club.

The picturesque village of Aylesford, with an ancient bridge over the River Medway four miles below Maidstone, was the scene of the famous battle which resulted in the Saxon conquest of Kent in the middle of the fifth century. It now attracts thousands of visitors through its narrow streets who come to see the Friars, the great Carmelite house standing on the banks of the river to which this religious order returned after a lapse of 400 years.

The Carmelite priory at Aylesford was founded in 1242 when Richard de Grey brought a group of hermits over from the Holy Land and gave them his manor at Aylesford. The community flourished and the priory was expanded and rebuilt. When the Reformation was brought in, the Friars, with the other religious houses, was suppressed and there was great indignation that Thomas Cromwell's agent at Aylesford in 1538 was a renegade friar, Richard Ingworth.

The property went to the Wyatts of Allington Castle but all they did was to demolish the church and living quarters and to use the stone for other buildings. When the Wyatts lost their properties in Kent as a result of their part in the rebellion the Friars was given to Sir John Sedley. He treated the place in a more kindly fashion, building another storey on to the medieval gatehouse and adapting the buildings into a comfortable country manor house.

When it became the property of Sir John Banks in the next century he carried out more improvements. His daughter married a Heneage Finch, who was raised to the earldom by George I for political services and, as he lived at the Friars, took as his title 'Earl of Aylesford'. However, this family soon acquired other estates and spent little time at Aylesford.

In recent times the Friars was owned by a family named Copley-Hewitt and during this period a serious fire damaged much of the building. One beneficial result of this fire was that it destroyed some of the rebuilt portions and uncovered the old cloister arches of monastic days. Work of restoration was held up by the Second World War when the Friars was occupied by troops.

In 1949, when the Carmelites arrived, the Friars was in a sad and sorry state with ivy climbing over the walls, windows boarded up and weeds across the lawns.

The work of restoration was begun and now the Friars is a handsome collection of buildings to which pilgrims flock in their thousands. It provides a place of retreat for people of all denominations, a conference centre and a pottery which produces a wide range of stoneware made by brothers of the community. There is much to be seen as the Friars is freely open to the public. The great courtyard has buildings dating back to the fifteenth century, the pilgrims' hall which entertained Edward II in 1325, cloisters, shrines and sanctuaries. There are memorials to two Carmelites who died in Nazi concentration camps.

The Friars stands on the River Medway and this can be a mixed blessing as the community discovered in 1965 when floods caused thousands of pounds' worth of damage. The old watergate, used by the friars for their journeys by river, is still as it was when Samuel Pepys visited it in 1669 and remarked, "I was mightily pleased with the sight of it."

It was a sad day for the Carmelites when they were thrown out of the Friars in 1538 but they have now returned to these beautiful old buildings in renewed strength.

Another monastic property given to the Wyatt family at the Reformation was Malling Abbey. It was originally founded by Bishop Gundulf of Rochester in 1099 but it and the village was totally destroyed in a disastrous fire in 1190. When rebuilt it was re-established as a nunnery for Benedictine nuns, one of the first in the country.

This nunnery seems to have run into financial difficulty caused by bad administration. In 1321 the abbess Joan, sister of Bartholomew de Badlesmere (whom we met at Leeds Castle), was the subject of an inquiry by the bishop and dismissed from her post. A few years later the bishop reported that the nunnery had been so ruined by bad administration "that it seems unlikely it could be repaired to the day of Judgement".

Stronger measures were taken to control the nunnery and it managed to survive until the Reformation in 1538. When the buildings were taken over by the Crown they were presented to the Cobham family but they lost them in 1603 for plotting against James I.

After passing through various hands an Anglican Benedictine community of nuns took over in 1916. Much of the abbey is still medieval with fine Norman windows. It was originally built of Caen stone and modelled on Rochester Cathedral. There is a splendid Norman tower, cloisters, fourteenth-century gatehouse and guest house.

The other Norman building at Malling is St Leonard's Tower, one of the earliest Norman keeps. This was also built by Bishop Gundulf and was part of his castle there. It stands 60 feet high but the top storey is in ruins.

It was once used as a prison and then as a hop storeroom, but is now cared for by the Department of the Environment.

The Neolithic period is represented in Kent by a number of megaliths in the Maidstone area. The best known is Kit's Coty on the slopes of Bluebell Hill, just off the Maidstone–Chatham road. This consists of three upright sarsen stones with another over them acting as a roof. It is thought to be the entrance to a long burial barrow, but this barrow has now disappeared under the ploughs of the farmers who have tilled this land for centuries. Whether it was a communal grave or the single grave of a famous leader is unknown. Another theory is that Kit's Coty is a false doorway erected to mislead thieves who might break into the tomb and steal the treasures buried with the dead.

Down the hill towards Aylesford is another megalithic monument which has collapsed into a jumble of huge stone slabs. These are known locally at the Countless Stones because no-one has ever been able to establish just how many there are. They sprawl one on top of another so that you are never sure whether a stone is a new one or you have already counted from the other side. Any number between twenty-one and twenty-eight may be correct.

Boughton Monchelsea Place, south of Maidstone with a glorious view over the Weald of Kent, can trace its ancestry back to Saxon times. It belonged to Earl Godwin, father of King Harold, who was killed at the Battle of Hastings. After the Norman Conquest it went to Odo, Earl of Kent, who lost it when he staged a rebellion against William II.

A family called Montchenies, from Mont Cenis in Normandy, took over the estate and gave their name to the second part of the name of the village which had up to then been known as Bocton. The family also held large estates in Norfolk, Suffolk and in other parts of Kent. They were responsible for providing the castle guard at Dover Castle. During the wars of Henry III and Simon de Montfort they were opposing the king and were lucky not to forfeit their estates. The Montchenies line died out when William de Montchenies was killed while directing mining operations at the siege of a castle at Drystwyn in Carmarthenshire in 1287.

Boughton Monchelsea passed through several hands until it was bought by Thomas Wyatt of Allington Castle in 1551. He held it for only a year before selling it, together with another manor at Wittersham, to his friend Robert Rudston for a fee of £1,730. The Rudston family occupied the estate from then right down to 1888.

Robert Rudston came from a Yorkshire family who had made their fortunes as drapers, bought land and moved up the social scale. His father had been Lord Mayor of London and Robert married Anne Wotton, daughter of the treasurer of Calais. The Wotton arms, united with the Rudston arms, can still be seen on the windows in the hall.

Rudston was persuaded by his friend Thomas Wyatt to join in his revolt in 1554 against the Spanish marriage of Queen Mary. When the revolt was crushed, Wyatt was executed and Rudston was sent to the Tower of London. His name can still be seen there, scratched on the wall of St John's Chapel in the White Tower. His estate at Boughton Monchelsea was confiscated but he managed to buy it back at a cost of £1,000 when he was released in the following year.

Boughton Monchelsea was then a medieval manor house about the size of the south-west corner of the present home and can be identified by the five mullioned windows. Robert Rudston greatly extended the property, lengthening the house and adding three more wings which enclose the courtyard. By 1613 it had a hall, a gallery, two dining-rooms, three living-rooms, fourteen bedrooms and kitchen and stores.

Rudston was well respected in the neighbourhood but seems to have quarrelled with his elder son for, when he died in 1590, he left Boughton Monchelsea to his younger son, Belknap. In his will he named William Lambarde as his executor. Belknap held the property until his death in 1613 and it then went to his sister Ursula who had married Sir Martin Barnham who owned other property at Hollinbourne and Bilsington.

Barnham represented Maidstone in Parliament for twenty-four years and when he died his son Robert, who was created a baronet in 1663, carried on as the M.P. for another nineteen years. He had been imprisoned in Leeds Castle by the Parliamentarians when he took part in the second civil war for the royalist forces in 1648. When Charles II regained the crown Sir Robert attended the coronation banquet and, as holder of the manor of Bilsington, performed the traditional duty of carrying in the last dish of the second course to be served, When he died in 1685 he left Boughton Monchelsea to his daughter Philadelphia who had married Thomas Rider, a city merchant.

Rider carried out alterations and extensions to the house but it appears that he and his son, Sir Barnham, were hard drinkers for Philadelphia, who died in 1730, left the sum of £400 to her twelve-year-old grandson Thomas "to educate him as a gentleman so that he might be sensible how fatal intemperance had been to his father and grandfather".

Thomas held Boughton Monchelsea for the next sixty years and considerably enlarged the property. He was High Sheriff of Kent and, at the coronation of George II, performed the traditional service for the manor of Bilsington by carrying the last dish of the second course. His improvements included the building of a brewery, bakehouse and a dairy and he made the estate practically self-supporting.

When he died in 1786 Boughton Monchelsea passed to his cousin, Ingram Rider of Yalding, and this family carried out the Gothic and Romantic architectural alterations which can still be seen. The windows in the dining-room contain the Rider arms, the Champney arms of his mother and the Carr arms of his wife. More bedrooms were added and the turret clock dated 1647 was moved to its present position. New gardens were also laid out.

His son, Thomas Rider, was Member of Parliament for West Kent and a great supporter of the Reform Bill of 1832. He commemorated the passing of the Bill by a memorial tablet in the hall of Boughton Monchelsea Place. When he died in 1847 the new owner, Thomas, decided to live in Wales and his descendant, who lived in the United States, came to Boughton Monchelsea and briefly looked over the estate, but apparently did not like it. Boughton was left empty for a number of years but was bought in 1903 by Lt-Col. G. B. Winch of the brewery firm of Style and Winch. He was succeeded by his nephew, Mr Michael Winch, the diplomat and journalist, in 1954.

The present house is built of ragstone from the local quarries which had in their time provided some of the stone for Westminster Abbey. During the Middle Ages the hard stone from these quarries had been used for making cannon balls. The stained glass in the windows has a curious origin. It was the gift of a German, Wilhelm Reiffgens, who had been well treated in the village when he had been there as a beggar.

Deer have been present in the park of Boughton Monchelsea Place for more than 300 years. A manuscript dated 1669 refers to land "enclosed and stocked with deere and conyes [rabbits] and used by Sir Robert Barnham as a park". There are now about forty head of deer in the park, from which one can look down over the rolling grassland almost to the sea 25 miles away.

6

The Medway Towns and the Isle of Sheppey

CHARLES DICKENS, although born at Portsmouth, was a true man of Kent. He loved the county and it is the setting for many of his novels.

Dickens spent his boyhood at Chatham, bought the house of his dreams nearby, spent his honeymoon at Chalk, near Gravesend, lived by the sea at Broadstairs where he owned another house, died in his favourite home and expressed a wish to be buried in Rochester Cathedral.

His father, John Dickens, was a Navy pay clerk on a salary of £110 per year when Charles John Huffham Dickens was born in February 1812. Four years later he was transferred to Chatham were they lived at No. 2 Ordnance Terrace. Here the little boy grew up and started to create from living persons the characters he would later use in his books. His father was the model for Mr Micawber, Miss Newnham, a neighbour, became the mad Miss Havisham in *Great Expectations,* and another neighbour, George Stroughill, would emerge in *David Copperfield* as Steerforth. The servant's surname was Weller, immortalized in *Pickwick Papers.*

Presumably nothing "turned up" for his Mr Micawber father, for the family had to move to a much smaller house in St Mary's Place. Living near the royal dockyard brought him close to ships and the sea, a subject which was to fascinate him all his life. He played games with his friends in a hayfield, now part of the railway station, and this field is remembered in *The Uncommercial Traveller* as having hawthorn trees, buttercups and daisies.

From his home he could see Rochester Castle and

Rochester Cathedral and this view is described in *Dombey and Son.* Mr Pickwick stood on Rochester bridge while waiting for his breakfast at the Bull, a hotel still there. It was a sad day for the eleven-year-old Charles when the family left the Medway towns for London where he was to experience misery when sent to work in a blacking factory.

Charles was often taken for walks in the area by his father and one of his favourites was over the bridge, through Strood and up the hill towards Gravesend. Here stood a house, Gadshill Place, which he much admired. His father, noting his liking for this rather grim-looking building, said: "If you were to be very persevering and were to work hard, you might some day come to live in it." The young Dickens always remembered Gadshill Place and, when he was forty-three and famous, bought it when it came on the market. He had written of it in *A Christmas Carol* as "a mansion of dull red brick, with a little weathercock-surmounted cupola the roof and a bell hanging in it".

Gadshill was built in 1778, the home of the local rector. Dickens embarked on a heavy programme of improvements. He put in a new drawing-room and two bedrooms, a study and a billiards-room. The coach house was converted into a servants' hall and a school-room made out of the loft. The shrubbery across the road was also in the property and here he built a conservatory connected by a tunnel to the house. The gardens were laid out with a croquet and bowls lawn and a deep well sunk to provide an abundant supply of water.

Dickens was a great walker and explored the area for miles around. He was particularly fond of the walk through the park of Cobham Hall to the Leather Bottle Inn which still preserves the Dickensian atmosphere. This inn is described in *Pickwick Papers* where the love-lorn Tracey Tupman consoled herself with a dinner of bacon and roast fowl. He went down to the marshes to Cooling (described in *Great Expectations*) and to Cobtree Manor on the Maidstone road, the Dingley Dell owned by the hospitable Mr Wardle where the Pickwickians spent Christmas.

On 8 June 1870 Dickens was at Gadshill working on *The Mystery of Edwin Drood* when he became ill. He died there on the following day. Although he had wanted to be buried in

Rochester Cathedral, his body was taken to Westminster Abbey to be interred in Poets' Corner.

Gadshill Place is now a school and Dickens would have liked to have known that two of his great-great-grand-daughters have been educated there.

Cobham Hall is a splendid Tudor mansion formerly owned by the Dukes of Lennox and Richmond. It stands in a fine park and gardens just off the motorway.

There was a manor on the spot at the time of the Norman Conquest. In 1208 the Cobham family moved in and amassed wealth by their profession of the law. In 1313 Henry de Cobham was created Lord Cobham and the 400 years of Cobhams at Cobham Hall was established.

John, the third baron, held other property in Kent. He built Cooling Castle, enlarged the nave of Cobham church and put up the tower. He also provided a new bridge across the river at Rochester to replace the old one which was in danger of collapsing. His grand-daughter Joan, who suc-ceeded him in 1407, was married five times (her fourth husband was Sir John Oldcastle, the Lollard) but only one daughter survived from these five marriages. She married into the Brooke family and her husband took the title.

William, Lord Cobham, a great favourite at the court of Queen Elizabeth, was responsible for the extensive building operations which transformed the manor house into a great Tudor mansion, but the reign of the Cobhams at Cobham Hall was coming to an end.

His son Henry, who succeeded to the title in 1596, was involved in the plot against James I to replace him on the throne by Lady Arabella Stuart. He was arrested, tried and sentenced to death but this was commuted to life imprison-ment. The estates of the Cobhams were forfeited to the king.

King James gave Cobham Hall and the estate to his second cousin, Ludovic Stuart, second Duke of Lennox. Soon afterwards he was created first Duke of Richmond and thus became the premier duke in both England and Scotland. As relatives of the royal family, the owners of Cobham Hall were important in national affairs. When Charles I married the French princess Henrietta Maria, he called in at Cobham Hall on his way back to London from Dover.

When the civil war broke out the Lennox and Richmond family naturally rallied to the support of the king. James, the fourth duke, fought with the royal army and came through the war unscathed but his three brothers were all killed. The estate was forfeited but James managed to compound with the Parliamentarians and was allowed to return to Cobham Hall.

Charles Stuart, sixth and last Duke of Lennox and Richmond, pulled down the old central portion of the house and built the splendid west front. His duchess, Frances, known as 'La Belle Stuart', was one of the most colourful and romantic figures in the Restoration era. She had spent her childhood in exile in France but returned to England with Charles II in 1660 and at the age of fifteen was appointed maid of honour to the queen, Catherine of Braganza. She was a noted beauty, a great favourite of the king, and it was said that if Queen Catherine had died when she was seriously ill in 1663 Charles would have married Frances.

When medals were struck to commemorate the naval victories in the Dutch wars, Frances was the model for the figure of Britannia. That design has been incorporated on coins of the realm down to the present day.

She was courted by the Duke of Lennox and Richmond but the king did everything he could to prevent the marriage. Life at court was not pleasant after the wedding in 1667 and so, with the queen's assistance, she fled from the Palace of Whitehall. Wrapped in a dark cloak she slipped out into the streets and across the river to a tavern where the duke was waiting for her.

For a time she was in disgrace at court but the king eventually relented and recalled her as Lady of the Bedchamber to the queen. After the duke's death in 1672 Frances sold Cobham Hall to her sister-in-law, Lady Catherine O'Brian. She had married Sir Joseph Williamson, a name still remembered in Rochester where he was a noted benefactor. Cobham Hall passed down the family until a female descendant married John Bligh of Rathmore, County Meath. He took over the estate and was quickly raised to the peerage and then, in 1725, created Earl of Darnley in the peerage of Ireland. This family did much to improve the property and John, fourth earl, who was a friend of Gainsborough and Reynolds, was responsible for collecting the famous paintings in the picture gallery. He also entertained the Duchess of Kent, the mother of Queen Victoria, at Cobham Hall in 1819. Writing of this event to his son, he said, "There is every prospect that HRH will speedily produce a healthy heir to the throne." He was right, for Queen Victoria was born three weeks later.

The Darnleys were renowned cricketers and the fourth earl and his brother were both members of the Kent team. There is a record of a match between Kent and Hampshire being played at Cobham Hall in 1792. The eighth earl, then the Hon. Ivo Bligh, is one of the great figures in the game. Following England's disastrous defeat at the Oval in 1882, it was recorded that "the body will be cremated and the ashes taken to Australia". This was the start of the series of test matches between the two countries for the mythical Ashes. The Hon. Ivo Bligh took a team to Australia that winter, won the series and regained the Ashes. At Melbourne a cricket stump was burnt, the ashes collected and placed in an urn and presented to the victorious English captain. The urn remained for many years at Cobham Hall but is now at Lord's Cricket Ground.

Cobham Hall is now a school and open to the public on certain days in the year. Visitors can see the Tudor wings erected in 1584 which completely transformed the old building. A special licence was obtained from the French king, Henry IV, to import 200 tons of Caen stone for the building. One room is now called 'Queen Elizabeth's Room' but this is a complete misnomer for, although she paid two visits in 1559 and 1573, this particular room was not built then. There has been a deliberate attempt to hoax the visitor with the inscription of Tudor dates by the architect, George Repton, who carried out alterations in the nineteenth century. On the ceiling he placed the date '1599'—presumably a mistake for the year of her first visit was 1559 when this part of Cobham Hall had not been built.

Cobham has always been famous for its gardens and this continues today with colourful displays of bluebells, flowering cherries, azaleas and rhododendrons. Many of the trees in the park are ancient and of enormous size.

This fine example of Tudor England is now well cared for

and represents the stately home of families who lived in a gracious and more leisurely age.

Unfortunately, the mausoleum erected for the third Earl Darnley in 1783 has fallen into decay. It is some way from Cobham Hall and not now connected with it. In the event it was never used as a mausoleum. Built of Portland stone it has red marble facings and Doric colums. It was designed as a magnificent building and this can be seen today even though it has been so shamefully neglected.

Chatham is famous for its Royal Naval Dockyard. There is a record of the fleet anchoring in the River Medway in 1547 when storehouses on the bank were hired at a cost of 13 shillings. The first ship built there was launched in 1585. The dockyard was enlarged and extended in Stuart times.

In 1667 the Dutch sailed up the Medway and inflicted a severe and humiliating defeat, but Chatham continued to be the main anchorage of the navy. The main buildings of the dockyard were erected in the eighteenth century and, although not normally open to the public, there are the odd occasions when it is possible to gain admittance.

The main gate is dated 1720 and has massive square towers. Just inside is the dockyard church erected in 1808. The Ropery is still used for making ropes. It is more than 1,000 feet long, open at both ends, and has a hemp store, a spinning room and a tanning house. Near here is the Admiral's House, a fine, brick-built building put up in 1703. It has a fine painted ceiling of Neptune crowning Mars.

The days of sail are recalled by the Sail Loft which still has the original benches and lockers of the old sailmakers. Nearby is the Mast House built in 1760.

In 1750 the dockyard covered 61 acres but, just over 100 years later, this had been extended to 500 acres with wharves extending to 10,000 feet. In recent years, with the decrease in the size of the fleet, the dockyard has shrunk to about half this size. Its heyday as a great naval base is past but there is much here to remind one of naval tradition and of the days of sail.

Facing the dockyard across the river is a Tudor castle which was built to protect it but which, on the only occasion it was attacked, failed humiliatingly to perform this duty. Upnor Castle was built in 1561 and is a three-storeyed building jutting out into the river with towers at each end, gun platforms and a stockade.

As soon as Queen Elizabeth came to the throne she ordered a castle to be built to protect the dockyard and the warships anchored in the River Medway. At that time twenty-three of the largest ships of the fleet were moored here and, without sails or rigging, would have been sitting ducks if an enemy fleet had raided up the river. Six acres of land belonging to a Thomas Devinisshe of Frindsbury was bought at a cost of £25 and Sir Richard Lee, the military engineer, designed the castle which was to stand upon it. The man responsible for the supervision of the building was Richard Watts, a former mayor of Rochester, who was victualler to the navy.

Watts kept the accounts during the building of the castle between 1559 and 1564. The largest payments were for the stone and wages for the masons and "hard hewers". Some of this stone came from the walls of Rochester Castle and other materials from the former religious establishments at Aylesford and Boxley. The woods of Sir Thomas Wyatt at Aylesford provided 90 tons of oak. In all £3,621 was spent on wages and materials, but a further £728 had to be spent in 1567 in providing the finishing touches. At that time 169 feet of glass was put in and the large sum of £253 was paid out for lead for the roof. The final touch was to erect a gilded lion to serve as a weather vane.

Following the execution of Mary, Queen of Scots there were grave fears that Spain would mount an attack. Ships were stationed off the Isle of Sheppey to protect the estuary and an iron chain was stretched across the river below the castle. This chain cost £80 a year to maintain. The castle had a garrison of eighty men who were paid 8d. per day.

In 1601 the castle was extended to include a timber palisade, a huge ditch and raised gun platforms. Again Rochester Castle was raided to provide the stone. A well 36 feet deep was dug and stables and lodgings erected at the back. All this cost £1,200. The armament of Upnor then consisted of a demi-cannon, seven culverins, five demi-culverins, a minion, a falcon, a saker and four fowlers. There were also thirty-four long bows which seem to indicate that, despite the introduction of gunpowder, these weapons still had their uses.

At the outbreak of the Civil War in 1642 Upnor Castle was garrisoned by Parliament and used as a prison for captured Royalist officers. When the Royalists in Kent rose in 1648 they seized the castle but this rising was quickly put down and the castle garrisoned again by parliamentary troops. Fairfax, the parliamentary general, carried out an inspection and ordered repairs to be made to the gun platforms and towers, and £673 was spent on these. This is one of the very rare instances in which the Parliamentarians repaired castles. It was their usual practice to demolish or damage them so that they could never again be used by the king or Royalists against the people.

After the Restoration came Upnor's first and last military engagement. War had broken out with the Dutch but, after a victorious battle at sea in 1667, it was thought that the enemy fleet had been so badly beaten that there was little to fear. The English ships were therefore brought back into port and sheltered behind land defences.

But the Dutch were not beaten and a squadron under Admiral de Ruyter sailed up the Thames, attacked and burned the fortress at Sheerness and sailed on to Chatham. The Duke of Albermarle rushed down from London to take charge and established guns along the river banks. The Dutch ships came through unscathed, charged the chain and broke it and anchored in the river until the tide turned. They quickly captured the warship *Royal Charles* and burnt other ships at anchor. As they came further on the Dutchmen came under artillery and musketry fire from Upnor Castle but were able to retire at leisure undamaged.

The diarist John Evelyn went down to Chatham to inspect the damage and recorded "as dreadful a spectacle as ever any Englishman saw and a dishonour never to be wiped off". A royal warrant ordered that Upnor Castle was in future to be kept up as "a fort and a place of strength". Samuel Pepys, Secretary to the Navy, was among the few who spoke up for Upnor and reported that it was lack of munitions and not lack of courage on the part of the garrison which was responsible for the disaster, but he had to admit that the fire from the castle had inflicted no significant damage upon the Dutch ships.

This humiliating defeat led to a review of the defences of English ports and huge sums were spent in putting up fortresses to protect Plymouth, Portsmouth, the Thames and the Medway. Forts were built further along the river towards Sheerness, for now that ships were larger they needed a deeper draught and had to be moored down river towards the sea. In spite of requests from the Admiralty, the chain, which had been broken by the Dutch, was not replaced.

These new measures reduced the importance of Upnor Castle as a defensive work. In 1668 it was downgraded to a storeroom and began another period of its history as a magazine to supply munitions to the navy. By 1691 Upnor had in stock 164 guns, 62 standing carriages, 100 ship's carriages, 7,125 round shot, 204 muskets, 77 pikes and 5,206 barrels of gunpowder. This role continued until 1827 when it became an ordnance laboratory.

Upnor Castle, as a magazine, was protected by a detachment of soldiers from the nearby barracks. In 1746 these soldiers were described as "a set of drunken wretches" and the storekeeper put in a requisition for a railing to be erected in front of the barracks to prevent them falling over the cliff.

Upnor Castle again became a magazine store in the Second World War when it was damaged by bombing. Restoration was carried out and it is now in the care of the Department of the Environment and freely open to the public.

By the bridge at Rochester stands a reminder of the other great military religious order, a manor house of the Knights Templars. Like the Knights Hospitaller at Sutton-at-Hone, the order was established in the Holy Land during the crusades to protect the holy places of the pilgrims. The knights were celibate soldiers living under stern monastic rules modelled upon the Cistercian Order. The Pope recognized their order in 1128, by exempting the Templars from interference by bishops or other ecclesiastical officials, except their own, in all the countries of the Christian world. These privileges caused the Templars to become unpopular with the church authorities and this was made worse by their solidarity and secret operations.

The Knights Templars soon acquired wealth and estates as rewards for the gallant fighting which they performed in the Holy Land. These estates were spread throughout Europe and the Templars had become a wealthy international body. They lent money to kings and nobles and were granted high offices in the country as they were respected as efficient business managers. Kings and queens were in their debt and it was probably to settle some accounts that Henry II gave the manor at Strood to the Templars.

The order already had a preceptory at Temple Ewell near Dover and Strood was convenient for the knights as a lodging on the way from London to Dover and the Continent. They had already established their own private postal service along this road. A fine stone building was put up and new lodgings for high officials of the order such as the Knight Templar who became the Royal Almoner of Henry III. This king became more and more in debt to the Templars and cleared some of them by remission of taxes.

By 1291 the Christians had been expelled from the Holy Land and the ostensible reason for the existence of the Templars had gone. They had become so unpopular that it was not surprising that there were moves to have the order suppressed. The first came from Philip IV of France who, having confiscated the possessions of all Jews in his country, then seized those of the Templars. All Knights Templars in his country were arrested and accused of all sorts of crimes. The Pope tried to protect them but, being to all intents and purposes the prisoner of Philip, was forced to submit.

Other countries quickly followed suit and in 1308 the Templars in England were arrested and imprisoned. By 1312 the order had been dissolved and the possessions of the Templars given to the rival military religious order, the Knights Hospitaller. Strood was at first held by the king, Edward II, and the property was shown as a hall, a chamber, a chapel and a barn. The Hospitallers rented out Strood for farming and do not seem to have occupied it themselves.

Strood Manor later belonged to the nunnery of Denny in Cambridgeshire and, as such, was confiscated at the time of the Reformation. It then went to the Cobham family and in Stuart times to the Duke of Richmond at Cobham Hall.

Passing through many hands, it was eventually acquired by the City of Rochester and is now owned by the Department of the Environment. It now stands in the middle of an industrial estate.

Strood Manor consists of a thirteenth-century stone building with shafts of Purbeck marble. The undercroft with its bays of ribbed vaulting is particularly impressive.

The keep of Rochester Castle which towers 113 feet above the River Medway is the highest in the country. It was built to guard this important river crossing where there was a battle when the Romans came in A.D. 43. There was even then a bridge of some sort over the river but the Ancient Britons destroyed it as the Roman army approached. The Romans then moved upstream to a point where their cavalry swam the river and then attacked the enemy from the rear.

The Saxons had a fort on the site but it was the Normans who built the present massive structure. Bishop Gundulf put up a castle in 1080 and, shortly afterwards in 1126, William de Corbeuil, Archbishop of Canterbury, erected the huge keep. The castle spread over an area of 160 yards by 130 yards guarded by curtain walls, but the keep is a square of 70 feet with walls 12 feet thick. This was the first of the great square keeps to be built in England.

There is an interesting account of how Gundulf came to build the castle. The manor of Haddenham in Buckinghamshire had been granted to the monks of Rochester soon after the Norman Conquest but when William II came to the throne it was necessary to seek confirmation of this grant from the new king. As Bishop of Rochester, Gundulf made the application but was told he would have to pay £100 for the concession. He protested that Rochester did not have the money but it was then suggested to him that the payment would be waived if he built a new stone castle at Rochester. He agreed and built the castle at a cost of £60 and acquired Haddenham which was worth £40 a year.

Gundulf was also responsible for building the White Tower at the Tower of London, the nunnery and St Leonard's Tower at West Malling and a number of churches in the Medway valley. He had been a monk in the abbey of

Bec in Normandy where Lanfranc, the Archbishop of Canterbury, had been the prior. He was appointed Bishop of Rochester and built his cathedral on the lines of Canterbury Cathedral.

No sooner was the castle built than it was put to the test. Bishop Odo rebelled against the new king and, with the support of a number of barons, attempted to put the Conqueror's eldest son Robert on the throne. Odo and the rebels took over Rochester Castle which they made their headquarters and resisted all attempts to oust them. The king collected an army and marched on Rochester but Odo left and went to Pevensey Castle. William followed and took the castle. Odo was forced to swear to yield up Rochester Castle to the king and was sent there under armed guard to tell the garrison to surrender. When they arrived the garrison troops rushed out of the castle, captured the escort and installed Odo as its captain again.

William was then forced to lay siege to Rochester and finally the garrison had to surrender and ask for terms. Odo was exiled to Normandy but then went with Robert on a crusade and did not return.

The next king, Henry I, appointed William de Corbeuil, Archbishop of Canterbury, as constable of Rochester Castle and he built the massive keep. The archbishops retained it until the reign of King John who directed it should be taken away from Archbishop Langton, his enemy, and given to the Bishop of Winchester, his supporter. Langton refused and the barons supported him by seizing the castle and holding it against the king. There were more than 100 knights in the castle under their leader William de Albini, together with archers and men-at-arms, and so it was a large garrison which defied the king.

John quickly mustered an army and marched on Rochester. He first destroyed the bridge to prevent the rebels getting any support or supplies from London and then settled down to the biggest siege seen in the country up to that time. It took him two months before the castle fell and showed the king to have more military ability than he is usually credited with. Great stone-throwing engines were brought into position to pound the walls of the castle. There were five of them and so they could maintain a ceaseless barrage day and night. A continuous fire was kept up by the archers and crossbowmen on the defenders.

Failing to batter a way in, the king resorted to mining. This was usually the best way to succeed when attacking a square keep without a protecting moat for the attackers could work almost unmolested at one of the corners where they would be shielded from the fire of the defenders. John's sappers tunnelled under the south-east tower, and supported it with pit props to shore it up until they were ready. They then poured in bacon fat, set fire to the lot and a whole section of the great tower came down.

This was not, however, the end of the siege for the defenders withdrew behind the cross-wall and continued to resist. Their supplies were now running short and they were reduced to a diet of horsemeat and water. Those not capable of fighting were pushed out and captured by the king's army. Eventually the rest were compelled to surrender but John was dissuaded from his threat to hang the lot. Only one man was hung, a crossbowman who had deserted from the king's army. The knights were sent to imprisonment in Corfe and other royal castles.

The lessons learned at the siege of Rochester Castle were put to good use when other castles were built. Towers at the corners were rounded and projected out from the walls so that defenders could fire on sappers engaged in mining operations. Moats were dug so that the miners' tunnels would become flooded. Machiolated turrets were constructed so that the defenders could drop missiles on to the attackers while remaining under cover themselves.

In the reign of Henry III in 1217 it had become urgently necessary to repair the damage done to Rochester by the siege. In the next twenty years £680 was spent on the castle and then a further £300 on digging a deep ditch to prevent mining operations. Breaches in the walls were repaired, a drawbridge put in over the ditch, and the south-east tower, which had been brought down by the mine, was reconstructed. It was now built in a circular form to allow a field of fire and the keep today has three square towers and this one circular tower which had been reconstructed.

There was a third siege of Rochester in 1264 at the time of the barons' war against Henry III. Rochester Castle was held for the king by Roger de Leybourne who had with him the king's nephew Henry. The castle was besieged by Gilbert de Clare of Tonbridge Castle who was later joined by Simon de Montfort. They entered the city on Good Friday and looted the cathedral but, out of respect for religion, remained quiet on Easter Sunday. On the following day they attacked the castle with siege engines. This was kept up for a week but the walls successfully withstood the bombardment. They started to dig a tunnel but had to abandon the siege when news was received that the king and his son, the Lord Edward, were marching to relieve the castle.

Although the castle had not fallen, it had suffered considerable damage and little was done immediately to repair it. A survey estimated that at least £3,333 would be needed to restore the castle to its original condition but it was more than 100 years later that work was put in hand.

Edward III gave orders for repairs to be carried out and this involved the rebuilding of the curtain walls, strengthening the keep, rebuilding the great hall and chambers and altering the main outer gate and drawbridge.

Rochester was captured by Wat Tyler and his rebels during the Peasants' Revolt but it would seem that the garrison was sympathetic and did not resist too strongly. Nevertheless some damage was done which cost £500 to repair. The age of castles was now drawing to a close and Rochester was being left to decay. It escaped action during the Civil War when it was owned by the Weldon family who had been given it by James I. Demolition had been suggested but, although stone from some of the walls went to the building of Upnor Castle, it was recognized that the keep was too tough a nut to crack. It was eventually bought by the City of Rochester and handed over to the Department of the Environment.

The great keep is now a shell but the visitor can climb right up to the battlements by the old circular stairs in the towers. On the first floor is the original entrance and the postern gate. The second floor had the great hall and the Norman chapel while the next storey gives access to the galleries above the great hall. There is another Norman chapel on the fourth floor with stairs to the battlements from which there is a fine view over the Medway towns and river.

The castle stands gaunt and square, proud of the resistance it put up in those stormy and uncertain times. Children now play in the gardens surrounding the keep from where great siege engines hurled their stones against the walls.

In the shadow of the castle stands Rochester Cathedral. The Bishopric of Rochester is the second oldest in the country having been founded by St Augustine in A.D. 604. Being so close to the estuaries of the Thames and the Medway, the cathedral suffered badly from the raids of the Danes and the Vikings. From time to time the building was damaged and the monks scattered. With the coming of the Normans, order was restored and that great architect-churchman Gundulf became Bishop in 1076 and reigned at Rochester for the next thirty-one years. He completely rebuilt the Saxon church in the Norman style of great stone pillars and arches but his church lasted for only ninety-nine years. In 1177 it was almost completely destroyed in a disastrous fire and had to be rebuilt.

Being so close to the castle, the cathedral also suffered when that fortress was being attacked. King John's soldiers damaged the fabric and stole valuables in the siege of 1215 and there was more looting when Simon de Montfort's army attacked the castle. The cathedral was also the target of the Puritan soldiers during the Civil War when statues, tombs and windows were broken and damaged.

The crypt is one of the finest in the country with a heavy ribbed vault dating back to the thirteenth-century. One tomb which escaped spoliation was that of Bishop John de Sheppey who died in 1360. It was concealed for many years behind masonry.

Rochester Cathedral is modest by comparison with other cathedrals, having a length of only 310 feet. Its central tower rises to a height of 156 feet. Its most famous shrine was that of the Scottish baker, St William of Perth.

In the Middle Ages there was great competition amongst the cathedrals, monasteries and abbeys for holy relics from which miracles would occur. Even the smallest bone of a saint was sufficient for it would attract pilgrims who would donate alms in the hope that a miracle would be performed which would benefit them. For years Rochester had no such relic, or what would be called today a super attraction or a good selling point. Boxley Abbey had its wonder-working Rood of Grace and Canterbury had the tomb of St Thomas Becket. Pilgrims flocked to these places and ignored Rochester. The monks felt that something must be done to put Rochester on the map. William of Perth provided the answer.

The baker was making a journey to Canterbury and spent the night in prayer with the Benedictine monks at Rochester. Continuing his journey next day, he was murdered by his servant. The body was brought back to Rochester Cathedral for burial and it was then observed that miracles occurred around his tomb. He was quickly canonized as St William of Perth. Pilgrims heard of the miracles, flocked to Rochester and donated alms at the tomb. Rochester was on the pilgrims' map and the monks were happy.

Lambarde tells the story in his book and castigates the Rochester monks in his typical fashion. "It was now high time to devise some way whereby the Priory and Church of Rochester might be relieved of penury," he says. "To what hard shift of saints these good fathers were driven and how easily the people were then deluded. Here he moulded miracles plentifully and mad folks offered unto him liberally."

Cooling Castle on the marshes between the Thames and the Medway has a magnificent machiolated gatehouse with twin towers. It was built by John de Cobham in 1380 for the defence of the coast against French and Spanish raids. This followed a savage assault by raiders who landed on the coast in 1379 and ranged far and wide, burning villages and towns on the Kent coast. The castle consisted of a large outer curtain wall with an inner ward and was partially surrounded by a dry moat.

Cobham fell foul of Richard II who banished him and seized the castle but it was restored to him when Henry IV took the crown. He was succeeded by his grand-daughter Joan, one of whose husbands was Sir John Oldcastle, the Lollard. Oldcastle shut himself up in Cooling Castle but he was captured and executed for his heretic leanings.

Cooling Castle saw action during Sir Thomas Wyatt's

rebellion against Queen Mary in 1554. His troops battered down the west wall of the outer ward, rushed the drawbridge and captured the inner ward. They then forced Cobham and his two sons to march with them to London but they soon escaped and got back to Cooling.

Fearing he would be blamed and possibly accused of helping the rebels, Cobham immediately despatched a letter to the queen. "With a force of 2000 men he laid battery to the gate of the castle with two great guns," he wrote. "He laid four other pieces of ordnance against another wall of the castle, sorely battering it and the gates. I had four or five men killed and others wounded. With the gates battered in and ammunition expended I was compelled to yield after six hours."

The letter did not save him, for the queen sent him and his sons to the Tower to remind them to do better next time. They were not released until the following year.

Cooling does not appear to have been fully repaired or used as a residence after that date, but it is worth making the journey along the narrow winding lanes to see its fine gatehouse.

On the right-hand tower is a copper plate with black writing which gives the reason for the building of Cooling Castle:

> Knoweth that beth and schill be
> That I am mad in the helpe of the contre
> In knowing of whyche thyng
> This is chartre and wytnessyng

This plate is now difficult to read for the weather has taken its toll over the years.

The Isle of Sheppey, named after its once-famous sheep, is rather a backwater and is now being heavily populated with caravans and camping sites. The naval dockyard at Sheerness was closed recently.

Sheppey once possessed a castle which was regarded as a model for its time and the latest in defensive works. It was Edward III who built the castle in honour of his wife and called it Queenborough. He decided there was a need for a fortress here to protect the estuary and designed this castle

with six towers and a moat. It was built in a hurry because
the coast was being threatened by French raiders.

The king ordered work to proceed by day and night and,
so that his carpenters, glaziers and plumbers could see to
work in the dark, 12,516 candles were provided. It was
completed in 1366 and 148 labourers were engaged to dig the
moat.

The town grew up around the castle and it soon had a
church, market square, houses and a wool house. Goods had
to be carried across the water and so a ferry was instituted.
Edward had used it for transporting material for his castle
and it was called Kingsferry, the name it still bears today.

Queenborough never saw any action and it was condemned by the parliamentary commissioners in 1650. The
great well of the castle was still used in the next century to
supply warships with "good, soft, sweet and fine water".
Little remains of the original structure now.

A Saxon nunnery was founded at Minster on the Isle of
Sheppey by Sexburga, Queen of Kent, in A.D. 670. At that
time there were more than seventy nuns in residence. Within
the next twenty years it was savagely raided by the Danes on
three occasions, the nuns were murdered and the church
looted. Being so near to the coast at that period it was
constantly in danger from the Danes. It had to be abandoned but it was refounded after the Norman Conquest.
Then it remained until the Reformation although the nuns
were given a bad report by a visiting archbishop in 1296. He
found them "quarrelsome, garrulous, hoarders of secret
money and neglectful of their vows". They were punished by
solitary confinement.

The remaining parts of the nunnery are now incorporated
into the church.

7

The Weald

THE WEALD OF KENT is a delightful area of countryside stretching from the Sussex border across to the coast where the North Downs run into the sea and form the famous white cliffs of Dover.

The area was formerly a vast forest (weald) (wooded country) and the names of the villages in the area give further clues to its original state. Many of them end in 'hurst' (a wood) such as Hawkhurst, Goudhurst and Sandhurst. Others end in 'den' (a clearing in the forest) such as Biddenden, Marden, Smarden and Benenden.

The Weald formerly formed an almost impenetrable barrier from London to the sea and when Harold marched to face William the Conqueror at Battle in 1066 he was forced to make a wide detour to reach the battlefield. The clearance of the forest started when Kent was a centre of the iron industry and trees were felled to make charcoal for the forges. When coal was discovered the iron industry in Kent declined and moved further north.

Given this start, more of the land was cleared for farming, which has prospered. The soil provides good crops and the proximity to the great market of London makes farming profitable. Although greatly changed from its original state, the Weald remains one of the finest stretches of wooded country in Britain. It also contains some of the loveliest houses in the county.

The romantic ruins of Scotney Castle, mirrored in the waters of its lily-covered moat, are familiar to all lovers of Kent. Photographs have appeared on calendars and in guide books for many years. It is the moats surrounding these castles which make them so attractive and Kent is fortunate in this respect. Leeds, Allington, Scotney and the Ightham Mote manor house are perfect examples of this, while another, Bodiam, has escaped just over the border into Sussex.

Scotney Castle, near Lamberhurst, has not been restored but rather was deliberately left to decay in order to enhance its picturesque features. A new house was erected on the hill above to accommodate the owners in the last century but fortunately the old castle was not used to provide the stone and become ruined, as has happened in so many other cases.

On the paths around the moat where the tourist gazes admiringly at the castle there once roamed the iguanodons, giant prehistoric lizards 20 feet tall. Fossilized impressions of their footprints have been found in the stone in the quarry. There are also traces here of the iron ore which fed the forges of the industry in the Weald. The railings around St Paul's Cathedral in London came from Lamberhurst.

The first manor at Scotney was owned by Lambert de Scoteni, a son of William Fitzlambert, Lord of Crowhurst. This was in 1137 and it was presumably one of the manors distributed to the Normans after the Conquest. The Scoteni family vanished from the scene in the next century when Walter de Scoteni was charged with poisoning Gilbert, Earl of Gloucester and owner of Tonbridge Castle, and his brother, William de Clare. He was found guilty and hanged at Winchester. This was the period of the revolt of the barons against Henry III and, following the defeat of Simon de Montfort, Scotney was taken over by the king.

In the reign of Edward II a John de Grovehurst was granted hunting rights over the manors of Courthope, Scotney and Apdale. On his death his widow married John de Ashburnham and their son Roger was responsible for building the castle. Roger soon became an important local official. He was a Conservator of the Peace in Kent and also served on the commission to strengthen and maintain the walls and dykes on Romney Marsh.

The castle was built in 1380. The French were active in raids upon Kent and Sussex and it was essential for anyone living near the coast to take strong defensive measures. In 1377 Rye, Winchelsea and Hastings had been sacked and burnt. Scotney and nearby Bodiam could be reached fairly easily up the River Rother and castles were necessary at both places.

Roger de Ashburnham's building at Scotney was designed as a fortified manor, strong enough to contain the enemy until other troops could arrive from Tonbridge Castle. There were rounded towers at each corner of the rectangular building, a curtain wall and fortified gatehouse. No licence to crenellate appears to have been issued, although this had always been insisted upon by the king in earlier times in order that his barons should not become too powerful. It is probable that this was dispensed with in view of the danger from the French raiders.

A mason named Stephen of Lamberhurst who had built the church at Boxley Abbey was employed at Scotney. The stone was obtained from a local quarry. The moat, over which was a drawbridge, was constructed by diverting the River Bewl and by building a dam to bring up the level of the water. The area in front was left in a marshy condition as an additional means of defence.

Roger died in 1392 and Scotney was sold for a sum of 200 silver marks to Henry Chichele, Archbishop of Canterbury. He gave it to his niece, Florence, who married John Darell, of Little Chart, near Ashford. The Darells were to hold Scotney for the next 367 years.

Scotney Castle would appear to have been well prepared to withstand a siege for in his will Thomas Darell, who died in 1558, left to his son "all my harness for war, javelings, pikes and all my sheaves of arrows and bills". His widow was to live at Scotney and to be provided with forty wagonloads of wood each year for heating purposes.

The younger Thomas became a Roman Catholic and, in those troubled times, just after the Reformation, decided to construct secret hiding places within the castle. These were to come in useful in later years. His daughter Mary was a source of trouble to him as she proposed to marry a staunch Protestant. Darell objected but the girl appealed to Sir William Cecil, Queen Elizabeth's powerful minister, and the marriage was sanctioned. Darell had to give up one of his farms as a dowry for his daughter.

The secret hiding places in Scotney Castle were used by the Jesuit priest Father Richard Blount who was chaplain there and used it as a centre for his missionary activities for the Roman Catholic Church. The Catholics, and in particular Jesuit priests, were under grave suspicion as enemies of the state following the threats made by Philip of Spain. The Jesuits were suspected of being sent in to act as a fifth column and were liable to arrest on sight.

Blount was one of a party of Jesuit priests who came into the country from Spain in 1591. In disguise, they claimed they were the survivors of the naval expedition to Cadiz which had been led by the Earl of Essex. They successfully managed to hoodwink the authorities, although questioned closely at the time.

Father Blount was at Scotney for seven years before his presence was discovered. Then the castle was raided by magistrates and their servants. Darell and the male servants were arrested and packed off to Newgate Prison. His wife and children were kept in protective custody at the house of one of the magistrates and one maid was left to take care of the castle. Blount and his servant lay concealed in a hole underneath the staircase as the search of the castle was made. They remained there for seven days and then, at the end of his tether, the servant emerged and allowed himself to be arrested. The magistrates left and Blount came out and resumed his normal life.

There was still some suspicion that Scotney harboured a Jesuit priest for the magistrates came back later in the year, in the week before Christmas. Darell had died in Newgate and Scotney was in the care of his wife. She and the children were confined to one room over the gatehouse while the search proceeded. On this occasion Father Blount and his colleague John Bray hid in a secret hole in one of the walls of the castle. After ten days they had still not been found but Mrs Darell, who had been allowed out, noticed that a length of cord from Father Blount's cassock was protruding from the door of the secret hiding place. She stood by the wall and managed to give a warning to the two men inside who quicky pulled in the cord. She was however, heard "talking to a blank wall". The searchers battered away at the wall but heavy rain forced them to call a halt until the next morning. Blount and Bray realized that they would be caught and decided to make a dash for it. During the evening they came out. Bray courageously rushed into the castle and gave the alarm that thieves were stealing the horses from the stables. Followed by Bray, who vanished in the darkness, the searchers rushed out to the stables. Father Blount swam across the moat, joined Bray and they made their escape. On the following day their hiding place was discovered but the birds had flown.

In Stuart times measures against Catholics were eased and William Darell, grandson of Thomas, was allowed to rebuild some parts of the castle. It is probable that at this time the secret holes used by Father Blount were filled in as they have never been found.

His building operations got him into debt but his brother Henry, who succeeded him, managed to pay this off and agreed to look after the six children. He was a Protestant and ordered that the children were to be brought up in the Protestant faith. The mother, a Roman Catholic, objected strongly, took her eldest son away and kept him in Scotney Castle. Henry had to present a petition to Parliament in 1640 which said

> Elizabeth Darell the widow, being a violent Romanist, hath conveyed her son home to her and will not suffer him to go back to school but keepeth one William Applebee a Popish school-master in her home at Scotney Castle to teach the said children Popery and to that end keepeth her outdoors locked up, the house being walled and double-moated about and keepeth the castle gates with guns and halberds terrifying people and employing only the said William Applebee only to buy and sell for her and manage her estate.

Apparently Mrs Darell died soon after, for the son succeeded to the estate and the family was sensible enough to avoid trouble in the Civil War. Although the Darells had lost money in expensive lawsuits they seem to have played a leading part in the social life of Lamberhurst and the surrounding area in the eighteenth century. There is a record of a party given at Scotney Castle when twenty-eight people sat down to dinner and fourteen to supper, but the reign of the Darells at Scotney was fast approaching its end. To pay off debts the castle was sold to Edward Hussey in 1778. It was then described as a mansion house "lately substantially repaired" with kitchen and pleasure gardens, an orchard, coachhouse, brewhouse, stables for eight horses, an "excellent mineral well of the same quality as that at Tunbridge Wells", and surrounded by a moat well stocked with fish and with a Chinese bridge over the river.

The Hussey family, who came from Staffordshire, were in the iron-smelting business and had an interest in the forge at Lamberhurst, named the Gloucester Forge following a visit from the Duke of Gloucester, Queen Anne's son. Edward Hussey was succeeded by his son, Edward, who was a famous cricketer. He was a member of the Kent team which played Surrey in 1773 and played for England and the M.C.C. During the period of Napoleon's threatened invasion he was commissioned and raised a Corps of Guides, men recruited especially for their local knowledge. When he died his son, another Edward, decided that life at Scotney Castle was not comfortable and embarked on building a new house on the estate.

This new house was completed by 1843 and was built from stone quarried on the site. In addition to keeping down costs, this also meant that the quarry thus formed would give a dramatic view from the terrace of the old castle down below in the moat.

Scotney Castle is now in the care of the National Trust and therefore open to the public. The old castle was inhabited by the estate bailiff until 1905 but parts of it were taken down to increase the romantic character and expose the medieval portions. The gardens are beautifully main- tained with a profusion of roses, herbs, trees and shrubs so that every season brings its own especial glories in the grounds.

Down the hill from Tenterden is Smallhythe Place, for nearly thirty years the home of one of Britain's greatest actresses. Ellen Terry bought the property in 1899 when she was at the height of her fame and it was here that she died in 1928.

Smallhythe was built about 1480 before the sea had receded from Romney Marsh. It served as a port house to what was then a thriving shipyard. Known then as The Farm, it became Smallhythe (Small Haven) when the waters went away. The repair dock has been excavated on the south side of the house and this dock was in use from the thirteenth century until the silting-up of the channel in the seventeenth, but, even in this century, goods have been brought by barge from Rye to Smallhythe. The waterway has now, however, shrunk to a narrow ditch.

The house is pleasantly situated just off the road in a garden of roses. It has stout timbers and a red-tiled roof. The house and contents have been carefully preserved and were presented to the National Trust by Miss Edith Craig as a memorial to her mother, Dame Ellen.

Ellen Terry was born at Coventry and made her first appearance on the stage at the age of nine in *A Winter's Tale*. It was in the years between 1878 and 1902 when she was regularly appearing with Sir Henry Irving that she was recognized as one of the greatest actresses ever to grace the English stage. In addition to Shakespeare, she appeared in plays by Ibsen, James Barrie and George Bernard Shaw. Her last performance was in Walter de la Mare's *Crossings* at the Lyric Theatre, Hammersmith, in 1925.

Smallhythe Place has an intriguing collection of objects associated with the actress and the stage. Her old make-up basket in which she kept her grease paints for make-up and the little satin ballet shoes she wore as a child are here. She was probably wearing these shoes when a trap-door was closed on her foot while playing in *A Midsummer Night's Dream*. Her toe was broken but, although in great pain, she finished her performance. For this courageous act her salary was doubled, but at that time (1856) it was only a matter of a few shillings.

In the dining-room are objects owned or associated with such famous stage characters as David Garrick, Sarah Siddons, Edmund Kean, Peg Wolfington, Sarah Bernhardt and Charles Kemble. Sir Arthur Sullivan gave her his monocle and scratched his autograph on the glass with a diamond ring.

Ellen Terry's costumes over a period from 1875 to 1925 are on display and include the famous beetle-wing dress she wore as Lady Macbeth in 1888. Most intimate of all is her copy of Shakespeare, worn by constant use and annotated in her own hand.

These priceless mementoes of the stage when great actors and actresses were acclaimed by West End audiences now rest in this lovely house in the Kent countryside.

Sissinghurst Castle is another which is not a castle at all. It owes its title to French prisoners-of-war who spoke of it as *le château* as they would of a manor-house in their own country. This was then translated into *castle* and the name stuck.

Sissinghurst was a fine Tudor mansion which was slowly decaying when it was rescued by Sir Harold Nicolson and his wife, Victoria Sackville-West, who created one of the loveliest gardens in the country.

In the twelfth century the area was known as Saxingherste and a manor was built by a family who took the name de Saxingherste. It would have been a substantial residence, for Edward I and his retinue stayed there for four nights in 1305 and kings always travelled with a multitude of retainers. The only relic of that house is the moat, for it was pulled down by the new owners, a family named Baker, in 1490.

A new house was put up of which the entrance range survives. In the centre of this the central arch and gatehouse were inserted a few years later by Sir John Baker. There were also domestic buildings, a great hall and a chapel which have now vanished.

Sir John Baker founded the fortunes of his family. He was Attorney General, Chancellor of the Exchequer and Speaker of the House of Commons in the reigns of Henry VIII, Edward VI and Mary I. He seems to have possessed a genius for survival in that troubled period and earned the title 'Bloody Baker'. Accused of inhuman persecution of Protestants during the reign of Mary, his reputation suffered considerably and the huge fortune which he amassed was put down to his misdeeds. At his death in 1558 at the age of seventy he left this fortune to his son, Sir Richard Baker.

Most of the house was demolished by the new owner and a magnificent mansion complete with tower was erected in its place. A few years after it was completed Queen Elizabeth paid a visit and stayed at Sissinghurst for three days. She was then making a leisurely progress through Kent and also had a large retinue and so Sissinghurst finances must have been strained to cope with the accommodation and feeding of these retainers.

Although Sissinghurst remained in the ownership of the Baker family for another 100 years, they made the mistake of backing the wrong side in the Civil War between King Charles and the Parliamentarians. Much of the family fortune was lost in supporting the royalist cause. When the last male Baker died in 1661 he left only four daughters. Two of these died childless and the other two moved away.

No-one now wanted Sissinghurst and it rapidly went downhill. Horace Walpole paid a visit in 1752 and found the house and park in ruins. It was then to suffer even more at the hands of French prisoners-of-war from the Seven Years War. The Government leased Sissinghurst as a prison and doors and windows were bricked up to prevent the prisoners escaping.

More than 3,000 Frenchmen were imprisoned in Sissinghurst, crowded together in this decaying house. Inscriptions on doors show that eighteen men were kept in a room only 18 feet by 16 feet, giving them only 16 square feet apiece, hardly enough room to put down a bed. There were numerous complaints about the food, short rations, lack of heating and the brutality of the guards. Disease was rife and the French reckoned that the worse fate to befall a prisoner was to be sent to Sissinghurst. Not surprisingly there were many escape attempts but very few succeeded, and these attempts resulted in both guards and prisoners being killed.

One of the officers in charge at Sissinghurst was Edward Gibbon, author of *The Decline and Fall of the Roman Empire*. He reported that "The duty was hard, the dirt most oppressive, through which the men from their wretched barracks had two miles to march every day. The inconceivable dirtiness of the season, the country and the spot aggravated the hardships of a duty far too heavy for our numbers."

The French vented their spite on the house and burnt the furniture, panelling, doors and window frames. In 1763 when the war ended Sissinghurst was almost a wreck and valued at only £300.

There is one reminder left of the stay of these unhappy Frenchmen in the area. A few miles away to the east three roads meet and this spot was called by the French *Les trois chemins*. This name was retained by the natives but corrupted into English as 'The Three Chimneys'. This name is still there as the name of a public house which has an inn sign of a French prisoner looking up at a signpost.

Sir Horace Mann, who now owned the estate, pulled down most of the house for building materials in 1800 and only the tower, the priest's house, the south wing and front range were left. Sissinghurst then suffered a further indignity by being used as the parish workhouse for the next sixty years. It was later turned into a farmhouse and farm labourers lived in the ruins of this fine Elizabethan mansion.

It was not until 1930 that a fairy godmother appeared and waved her wand to save Sissinghurst Castle. Victoria Sackville-West, the author and direct descendant of Sir John Baker whose daughter Cecily had married Thomas Sackville of Knole, was looking for a new house where she could create a garden. She saw Sissinghurst Castle – "some high Tudor walls of pink brick remained as the anatomy of the garden-to-be". She saw the possibilities but had to admit to the drawbacks.

> The major nuisance was the truly appalling mess of rubbish to be cleared away before we could undertake any planting at all. The place had been on the market for several years since the death of the last owner, a farmer, who naturally had not regarded the surroundings of an old castle as a garden, but merely as a convenient dump for his rusty iron, or as allotments for his labourers or as runs for their chickens. The amount of old bedsteads, old plough-shoes, old cabbage stalks, old broken-down earth closets, old matted wire and mountains of sardine tins all muddled up in a tangle of bindweed, nettles and ground elder, should have sufficed to daunt anybody.

Nevertheless she fell in love with Sissinghurst. "It was Sleeping Beauty's Garden – a castle running away into sordidness and squalor; a garden crying out for rescue. It was easy to foresee even then what a struggle we should have to redeem it."

Sir Harold Nicolson designed the layout of the garden which was to be a combination of long axial walks running north, south, east and west. The garden was planned to have seasonal features so that there were always flowers from March to October.

It was a formidable task which they faced. There was no

water except from the wells, light was provided by oil lamps, all windows were broken and most of the doors missing. Until one of the cottages could be made habitable they camped out on the first floor of the tower. Gradually some sort of order was established. The stables were converted into a library, the roof completely renovated and the priest's house repaired. It resulted in an odd place as a residence. Each person had a separate building and had to walk, summer and winter, across the garden to sleep, eat, bath and work. The priest's house had the dining-room and kitchen, the children lived in the long building. Victoria Sackville-West's sitting-room was in the tower, and Harold Nicolson used the south cottage as his study.

Victoria Sackville-West died in 1962 in the priest's house, Harold Nicolson in 1968, and Sissinghurst Castle passed to the National Trust.

The towers have seventy-eight steps in the spiral staircase leading up to the roof. The right-hand turret had Victoria Sackville-West's sitting-room on the first floor where she worked on her many books from 1931 to 1962. Her books still line the walls. The top floor of this tower was used by the Home Guard in the Second World War.

It is the gardens and grounds which are the glory of Sissinghurst Castle. They remain as a tribute to Harold Nicolson and Victoria Sackville-West who rescued this old manor house, restored it and created one of the loveliest gardens in the country.

The village of Charing, nestling beneath the North Downs, once possessed a magnificent palace. This was one of the chain owned by the Archbishop of Canterbury. The others were at Otford, Wrotham and Maidstone which meant that the travellers could proceed at a leisurely pace of about twelve miles a day between these palaces. On the dreadful roads of those times this would have been as much as man and beast could travel in a day.

Charing came into the possession of the archbishops as early as 788. It was Archbishop Stratford in 1340 who built the great palace. This would have been of some considerable size for it accommodated Henry VIII and his retinue on his way to the Field of the Cloth of Gold. At the Reformation the palace was leased to private tenants but it was never kept in a state of proper repair and the buildings started to decay.

The palace is now part of a farm. All that remains is the gatehouse, porter's lodge, some domestic buildings and the great hall which is now used as a barn. A sad end to a palace which had known kings and clerics and the splendour of those days.

The lovely village of Goudhurst had its moment of glory in 1747 when it won a battle with a notorious gang of smugglers who had threatened to burn down the village and murder all the inhabitants. The Hawkhurst Gang, who transported the smugglers' cargoes inland, terrorized the Weald of Kent with acts of atrocity, robbery and murder. Goudhurst decided that the time had come to end this reign of terror and formed the Goudhurst Militia to put down the gang. An ex-soldier named Sturt was put in command and a declaration was drawn up expressing the intention of the villagers to fight the smugglers. The Hawkhurst Gang got wind of this move, captured one of the villagers and tortured him until he revealed the scheme. He was then sent back to the village with a message that the gang would attack on a certain day, murder all the villagers and burn down the village.

Goudhurst put itself in a state of defence. Weapons were gathered together, lead melted down to make balls for the muskets and barricades thrown up. True to their word, the smugglers attacked and opened fire. They were answered with a fusillade of shots which killed two of their number and wounded four others. Sturt's men kept up the fire and the Hawkhurst Gang turned tail and fled. The villagers had won the Battle of Goudhurst.

After the particularly brutal murder of two Customs officers the gang was captured and brought to trial. Sixteen were sentenced to death and the body of their leader, Thomas Kingsmill, was hung in chains at Goudhurst, the village which had stood up to the gang.

The magnificent gates at the entrance to Eastwell Park are now the only items of note in this once great estate. They now guard farmland and woodland, for Eastwell Park is no longer the stately home it was for hundreds of years. The "very noble mansion" erected in 1546 has gone, torn down and replaced by a building in Tudor style in between the wars. The splendid artificial lake is covered with reeds and inhabited by water fowl and the fine deer park converted to farm land.

Eastwell Park, once described by Daniel Defoe as the finest he had ever seen, was presented by William the Conqueror to Hugh de Montfort. In Stuart times it was held by the Earls of Winchelsea who remained there until 1900. One of these opposed the Duke of Wellington on the question of Catholic emancipation and their correspondence led to the duke issuing a challenge to a duel. They met in Battersea Fields in 1829. The duke fired first and missed and the earl fired into the air. They then made up their quarrel and became friends.

Eastwell was leased to Alfred, Duke of Edinburgh, in 1878 and he built the splendid gatehouse which bears his coat of arms. His daughter Marie, who became Queen of Rumania, was born at Eastwell.

There is, however, one very good reason for visiting Eastwell. By the side of the lake are the ruins of Eastwell church which was destroyed when it was hit by a V2 during the war. (How strange that this little church standing in the peaceful woods beside the lake should suffer in this fashion.) In this church is a tomb which is reputed to be that of Richard Plantagenet, illegitimate son of Richard III.

The story came to light in the eighteenth century when the then Earl of Winchelsea was examining the Register of the Parish of Eastwell and found the entry "Richard Plantagenet was buried the 22nd daye of December 1550". It was when Eastwell Park was being rebuilt in 1540 that the owner, Sir Thomas Moyle, noticed that one of the bricklayers would be reading a book during his leisure moments but hid the book when anyone approached. Sir Thomas crept up and surprised him and saw that the book was in Latin. Few people in those days could read or write and so Sir Thomas questioned his bricklayer. Then the story emerged.

The bricklayer said he had been brought up in the home of his nurse whom he took to be his mother. When he was seven he was sent away to a Latin schoolmaster and taught to read and write. He was well cared for but had no family and his only visitor was a gentleman who came to the house once a quarter to pay his board and to supply his needs. Once he was taken away on a visit to a great house where a great personage, finely dressed and wearing the Star and Garter, spoke kindly to him and gave him ten gold pieces.

One day, when he was sixteen the same gentleman came and said they must go on a journey. They rode to Leicestershire and, on Bosworth Field, he was taken to the tent of King Richard. The king embraced him and told him he was his father. "But, child, tomorrow I must fight for my crown," said the king. "Assure yourself that if I lose I will lose my life also. Stand in such a place where you may see the battle out of danger. When I have gained the victory come to me and I will then own you to be mine and take care of you. But if I should lose the day, shift as well as you can and be sure to let no one know that I am your father for no mercy will be shown to a son of mine."

The king gave the boy a purse of gold and next day was killed in the battle which gave Henry Tudor the crown. When the boy saw that the battle was lost he rode to London, sold his horse and fine clothes and had himself apprenticed to a bricklayer. He retained his fondness for reading and spent his spare money on books. His father had given him sound advice for Henry Tudor soon dealt with the remaining Plantagenets. The two sons of Edward IV, the 'princes in the Tower', were never seen again (whether they were murdered by Richard or Henry or died natural deaths has never been proved). The Earl of Warwick, Richard's nephew, was beheaded and another illegitimate son, John of Gloucester, clapped into prison where he died.

But Richard Plantagenet lived quietly working as a mason at Eastwell Park and never revealed his identity until he was nearly seventy. Sir Thomas offered to pension him off and take him into the house but Richard asked to be allowed to build a one-roomed cottage and to live there with his books until his death.

It must be a moving experience for those who do not believe that Richard III was the monster depicted by Sir Thomas More and by William Shakespeare to stand beside this tomb in the ruined church. Illegitimate or not, this

Richard was the last of the Plantagenets, a royal house which ruled England for 331 years, longer than any other royal line. He had survived the reigns of Henry VII and Henry VIII to die in this peaceful park at the age of eighty-one.

Godinton Park, on the outskirts of Ashford, is famous for the wood carving in the rooms. Most of this was executed by the exiled Huguenots.

Godinton was in possession of one family, the Tokes, for more than 500 years. The Tokes were reported to be descended from the Sieur de Touques who fought with the Normans at Hastings. It was in 1440 that the Tokes came to Godinton. A John Toke was rewarded by Henry VII in 1495 for his work at the French court in persuading Charles VIII not to support the pretender, Perkin Warbeck. The roof of the great hall of the building at that time is still there.

During the Reformation another John Toke served as a commissioner of inventory for church lands. He was accused of complicity in the Wyatt rebellion against Queen Mary and was imprisoned in Rochester Castle but managed to survive.

In 1627 Godinton was owned by Captain Sir Nicholas Toke who married five times but did not produce a son. His fifth wife was the daughter of the Earl of Winchelsea of Eastwell Park. Although a royalist captain he seems to have escaped lightly when Parliament eventually triumphed. He left the estate to his nephew, Nicholas, when he died in 1680.

The last of the Tokes left Godinton in 1895. The present owner, Mr Alan Wyndham Green, has preserved this historic property which is now in the sixth century of continuous occupation.

The great hall, dating from the fifteenth century, originally had a fire in the centre of the floor with the smoke escaping through a hole in the roof. This roof with traces of soot from the fire is still there but hidden by a ceiling put up by Captain Sir Nicholas Toke in 1630. There is some splendid wood carving in the great hall and seventeenth-century furniture. The great chamber or drawing-room has wood panelling dating from the seventeenth century and a chimney piece of Bethersden marble. The surrounds bear the arms of the Toke family, representations of Adam and Eve and a demonstration of musketry and pike drill.

In the park are the remains of the Doomsday Oak which is said to have been there since Norman times. On 3 September 1939, when Neville Chamberlain was announcing over the radio that Britain was at war with Germany, this great tree suddenly split down the middle and collapsed on to the ground.

Down the road towards the coast, behind Folkestone racecourse, are the scanty remains of Westenhanger Castle. It is squeezed in between the railway and the grandstand.

It was a square building with towers at the corners surrounded by a moat. Some parts of the walls are still standing, together with one of the towers and part of another.

Westenhanger was originally a manor house but a licence to crenellate was issued in 1343 to John de Kiriel. He put in a drawbridge and portcullis, fortified the battlements and added turrets. This was in the period when the French were raiding the coast and Westenhanger, only three miles from Hythe, would have been vulnerable. The castle had 126 rooms and 365 windows. Queen Elizabeth stayed there during her progress through Kent in 1573.

Used as a prison for captured parliamentary soldiers by the Kentish royalists during the Civil War, most of Westenhanger was pulled down in 1701 and the stone carted away for building materials. The tower which remains is known as Fair Rosamund's Tower after Rosamund Clifford, the mistress of Henry II. There is a legend that she was kept there before being sent to Woodstock.

At Aldington on the hills above Romney Marsh lived Elizabeth Barton, the 'Holy Maid of Kent'. She was a servant in the house of Thomas Cobb of Aldington when she started to make pronouncements on the state of the country which she said were divinely inspired.

The parish priest, Richard Masters, and a monk from Canterbury, Martin Bocking, decided to make use of the girl for their own ends. They directed her to say that miracles and restoration of health would be performed at the chapel at Court-at-Street, near Aldington, and that "Our Lady has appeared to me and told me so".

The fame of the Holy Maid and the chapel at Court-at-Street spread rapidly. Bocking, Masters and the Canterbury monks encouraged her to make other pronouncements, but when she forecast that King Henry VIII would lose his kingdom if he married Anne Boleyn, her fate was sealed. She, Bocking, Masters and the others were arrested and confessed. Elizabeth admitted that she had never had any visions and Bocking and Masters admitted that they had used the girl for their own purposes.

Elizabeth and Bocking were executed at Tyburn but Masters was strangely pardoned and returned to Aldington. In a pathetic speech from the scaffold Elizabeth said, "I am not so much to be blamed considering that it was well known to those learned men that I was a poor wench, without learning, and therefore they might easily have perceived that the things that were done by me could proceed in no such sort. But their capacities and learning could right well judge from whence they proceeded and that they were altogether feigned. But because the thing which I feigned was profitable to them, therefore they much praised me and bore me in hand that it was the Holy Ghost and not I that did them."

It is a story which brings little credit to the monks of Canterbury who encouraged the poor girl along the road to self-destruction. The little chapel, roofless and in decay, can still be seen. The path to it was once thronged by pilgrims but it is now muddy and overgrown.

Lympne Castle occupies a magnificent position on the edge of the hills and from it can be seen Romney Marsh and the sea along to Dungeness. There is evidence that there was a Roman watchtower on this site from where the sentry could see the harbour of the Roman Portus Lemanis, up the military road which ran straight to Canterbury, out to the sea from whence came the Saxon pirates and also be within hailing distance of the Roman castle below.

Lympne Castle originally belonged to the Archbishop of Canterbury and was occupied by the archdeacons. The old manor house was fortified as a defence in the time of civil war and also against the French raiders in the Hundred

Years War. Although the present castle dates from 1360 parts of it are much older. It remained fortified and garrisoned until the Tudors abolished the power of the barons and brought in more peaceful times.

The archdeacons now leased it out and there is a record of 1641 that it was bringing in a rent of £30 a year. It was used as a farmhouse and was eventually sold in 1860, the first time it had passed out of the possession of the archbishops of Canterbury since the Norman Conquest.

The castle was starting to decay but in 1905 the new owner commissioned Sir Robert Lorimer, the famous Scottish architect, to restore it to its former state.

During the Second World War it was again used as a watchtower and sentries were installed to watch for German invaders from across the sea from the same spot used by the Roman sentries nearly 2,000 years earlier.

Lympne Castle has undergone a number of changes over the years. The Great Hall was converted into a house by fitting a first floor halfway up its walls. The earliest part of the building is the square tower which dates from the thirteenth century and has walls five feet thick. The building was modernized in 1420 and the Great Tower with a newel stairway built on.

Lorimer took down the floor from the Great Hall to restore it to its original condition and this is one of the finest of its period in the country. The windows were fitted with new tracery and new windows were pierced to provide more light.

The concrete structure, put up by the army in the Second World War as a watchtower, was on top of the East Tower. It was felt that this was out of keeping with the medieval structure of the castle and should be removed, but it was preserved as being part of the history of the castle. It also provides a fine, draught-free vantage point from which to look over Romney Marsh to the sea. Lympne Castle is open to the public on certain days.

Down the hillside are the remains of the old Roman castle of Stutfall, one of the great fortresses controlled by the Court of the Saxon Shore as a defence against the Saxon raiders. In those days the sea came up to the walls and the Roman fleet anchored here in their Portus Lemanis. The foundations of a wall, with steps leading down to the quay and a huge ring to which boats were tied up, have been found.

Stutfall was a large fort measuring 250 yards by 250 yards. The walls were 20 feet in height and 12 feet thick and the whole area covered 10 acres. The fort had the usual Roman buildings, garrison headquarters, baths, storerooms and barracks.

Stutfall (the name means Stout Wall or Fortress) seems to have been abandoned as a result of landslides, before the Romans left Britain. By the time of the Norman Conquest some of the walls had tumbled down and Archbishop Lanfranc used the stones to build Lympne Church and Lympne Castle. Excavations carried out now show the outline of the fortress. The main entrance gate on the east wall was 12 feet wide and flanked by strong towers.

Enough remains of the walls bonded by immensely strong cement to give the visitor a clear impression of this Roman fort which commanded the Roman harbour. Today the sea has retreated and left Stutfall isolated on the hillside.

8

Canterbury

THE COAT OF ARMS of Canterbury, which are now more than 600 years old, symbolize the city's position as a royal city and the religious centre of the country. At the head of the shield is one of the lions from the Royal Arms of England and on it are three choughs or beckets, the device of St Thomas Becket of Canterbury. The motto is *Ave Mater Angliae* – Hail, Mother of England.

The magnificent cathedral towers above everything but Canterbury is not just a cathedral city. It has the oldest Christian church in the country, one of the earliest Norman castles, city walls and a splendid gate, Roman remains and a monastery founded by the great St Augustine.

Kings, queens, princes and archbishops are buried here and it once held the most holy and renowned shrine in the land before Henry VIII disturbed the bones of St Thomas Becket. It was the birthplace of Christopher Marlowe, who, some people claim, was the real author of the Shakespeare plays. At one time it held the royal mint and the coins produced then can be seen in the museum. There is even one of the first railway engines built by George Stephenson, appropriately named *Invicta*, the motto of the county.

For the serious student of history or the casual visitor there is much to see. Canterbury was bombed by the Luftwaffe in the so-called Baedeker revenge raids but the cathedral and most other historic buildings escaped serious damage. More than 400 high explosive bombs and 10,000 incendiaries were dropped on the city causing the deaths of 115 inhabitants and the destruction of 800 houses and buildings.

Compared to the destruction wrought in other cities one is thankful that it was no worse and that much of Chaucer's Canterbury is still there for us to enjoy. There was one beneficial effect of the bombing in that it enabled more excavation to be done, thus revealing more facets of the city's history.

There was a settlement in Canterbury long before the Romans came. Traces of a pallisade and a ditch from the Iron Age came to light after the bombing and also the remains of some wooden huts of the Belgic era. Canterbury is probably unique among cities in this country with evidence showing that it has been continuously occupied since the days of the Ancient Britons.

The Romans, when they came to stay in A.D. 43 colonized Canterbury (which they called Durovernum) and made it the important junction from their ports at Reculver, Richborough, Dover and Lympne. From here Watling Street went straight to London. It was apparently a pleasant residential town with fine houses, public baths and other amenities.

When the Romans left, Canterbury was exposed to the raids of the Norsemen from the sea and the attacks of the Celtic tribes from the north. King Vortigern of Kent made the mistake of inviting the Saxons into the country to fight off the Celts. They did this but then refused to leave. Hengist routed the Britons and took over the kingdom of Kent.

More Saxons and Jutes came in and Kent was soon a Saxon kingdom. It was a pagan land worshipping heathen gods until the arrival of St Augustine in A.D. 596, Queen Bertha, wife of King Ethelbert, was a Christian for she had come from France and brought her chaplain with her. St Augustine was received by King Ethelbert – out in the open so that no black magic could be performed – and was allowed to set up a church and conduct his missionary work. Soon afterwards King Ethelbert became a Christian.

St Augustine had landed at Richborough with forty monks who walked into Canterbury chanting litanies and bearing a silver cross. King Ethelbert gave up his palace at Canterbury to the monks and went to live at Reculver. On the site of the palace St Augustine established the Cathedral of Christ Church and, outside the city walls, founded the monastery of Saints Peter and Paul which was later to be called St Augustine's Abbey. There was to be intense rivalry and hostility between the cathedral and this abbey in the years to come.

Canterbury and the rest of Kent suffered under the ravages of the Danes in the tenth century in spite of paying Danegold to keep them away. Some of the church plate had to be melted down and sold to find this money but the Danes kept coming back for more. In 1009 they exacted the sum of £3,000 from Kent. Two years later they were back again, Canterbury was sacked and Archbishop Alphege taken prisoner The citizens were massacred and the monks took refuge in the cathedral. The Danes set fire to the building but the monks stayed inside until the molten lead began to drip from the roof. They then came out to meet their deaths.

Archbishop Alphege was carried off by the Danes and used as a bargaining point to exact further ransom. Alphege refused and was murdered at Greenwich, and became the first martyr of Canterbury. His body was brought back to the cathedral by King Canute in 1023.

There are now no traces of St Augustine's cathedral for it was reduced to a shell by a disastrous fire in 1067. The new Norman archbishop, Lanfranc, had to make use of a temporary wooden building when he was enthroned in 1070, as he found the cathedral "reduced almost to nothing by fire and ruin". He therefore set out to build a new cathedral – "a more noble one". He completed it in seven years. Much of the building material was the famous Caen stone.

Lanfranc was a great church administrator. He recovered the lands belonging to the cathedral which had been seized by Odo, Earl of Kent, and then settled the old problem of supremacy by securing that Canterbury had preference over York. The document recording this is still preserved in the Cathedral library.

When Lanfranc died William II was on the throne and so no successor was appointed as the king seized the revenues from the estate. William became ill and, fearful of death, quickly appointed Anselm as Archbishop to intercede with God for him. He later recovered and told Anselm he wanted the cathedral revenue back again. Anselm left the country and lived in Rome until the king was killed by an arrow while hunting in the New Forest.

Rebuilding had continued and in 1130 the Norman

cathedral was consecrated in the presence of Henry I and King David of Scotland. Anselm had returned to Canterbury and had obtained from the king the undertaking that bishops should be appointed by the Church although they could do homage to the king as a token for the occupation of land belonging to the Crown. It was at this period that the magnificent Norman crypt, which still survives, was built.

When Henry II came to the throne in 1154 he had decided on a policy of unifying Church and State and thus depriving the Church of the many concessions it enjoyed. He was also determined to end the practice under which priests and lay persons attached to the Church were dealt with in their own courts and not subject to the law of the land. Any cleric accused of any crime except treason could plead "benefit of clergy" and escape trial in the courts. The ecclesiastical courts were known for their leniency and only if the cleric was unfrocked could he be dealt with in the courts of the land. Henry felt that crimes by these "criminous clerks" should be properly punished.

The man he selected to implement this policy was Thomas Becket, son of a wealthy London merchant, who was ambitious and saw that the way to high office was by the Church. He was appointed to the staff of Archbishop Theobald of Canterbury and soon rose to be Archdeacon of Canterbury.

At the age of thirty-six he was appointed chancellor to the king and he and Henry became close friends. They both enjoyed the good things of life and Becket wore fine clothes, kept a fine stable of horses and was a generous host noted for his love of good food and wine. He fully supported the king's policy against the Church and, when the archbishopric fell vacant in 1162 Henry seized the chance of appointing his friend to the post. Now that Becket was Archbishop of Canterbury there could be no further obstacles to his policy of unifying Church and State.

He was to be sadly shocked and mistaken. Becket had accepted the post with some reluctance. On being consecrated on 3 June 1162 he resigned his office of chancellor saying that he could not serve God and the king. He adopted the life of a monk, lived in seclusion, wore a hair shirt next to his skin and, as he said himself, "changed from being a patron of play actors and a follower of hounds to being a shepherd of souls".

Henry was furious at what he regarded as this act of treason on behalf of his erstwhile friend. Quarrels broke out between the two on minor matters but then on the more serious question of the trial of members of the clergy. Henry pointed out that clerics in minor orders, found guilty of serious crimes, had escaped with light sentences in the ecclesiastical courts and he maintained that they should have been handed over to the lay courts where they would receive the same punishment as other people. Becket, who had previously supported this policy, now objected. Henry summoned him to the Council of Clarendon where the whole matter was thrashed out. After a bitter struggle Becket was forced to give way and it was decided that no appeal could be made to the Pope in Rome without the consent of the king, clergy were not allowed to leave the country without the king's approval, and the Church no longer had the power to protect convicted priests. These were embodied in the Constitutions of Clarendon to which Becket agreed although he refused to affix his seal to them.

This had not settled the quarrel between king and arch-bishop. Becket continued to support the trial of clergy in ecclesiastical courts and the king realized he would have to get rid of his rebel archbishop. Becket was suddenly summoned to Northampton to stand trial on a number of charges alleging that he had not kept proper financial accounts when he was chancellor. These were obviously trumped-up allegations designed to ruin Becket and he strongly defended himself. It was suggested that he should resign his office rather than face imprisonment and mutilation. When the Earl of Leicester started to announce the sentence on the archbishop he was cut short by Becket, flourishing his great cross, crying out: "No nobleman can judge a bishop, nor the king, nor the king's spokesman. I will be judged by our Lord the Pope alone, for he alone is competent to judge me and to him, in your presence, I appeal."

Two days later Becket fled to France and in the Abbey de St Bertin near Clair-Marais started his operations to thwart the designs of King Henry upon the English Church. Envoys were sent to the Pope who suggested Becket should retire to a monastery to consider his future actions. Becket became a monk at the Cistercian abbey of Pontigny where he adopted the harsh rule of the order. Henry was still able to harass his archbishop for he warned the Cistercians that if they continued to harbour Becket at Pontigny he would confiscate all Cistercian property in England. Becket then moved on to a Benedictine monastery near Sens. He retaliated against Henry by excommunicating a number of knights and officials who had supported the king against the church.

A position had now been reached when both sides were able to inflict injuries upon each other from long range and the Pope, seeing that the Church would suffer, attempted to mediate. He saw both Henry and Becket but neither would give way and the king even said, "I hope to God I never set eyes on a cardinal again." Nevertheless a meeting was arranged between the two antagonists in 1169 at Montmirail but they quarrelled immediately and left damning each other.

In the following year there was another meeting at Freteval near Chartres and this time, rather surprisingly, they met as friends. Henry said: "Since I find the Archbishop well disposed towards me, I would be the worst of men if I were not well disposed towards him."

It was agreed that Becket should return and take up his duties as Archbishop of Canterbury and he arrived back on 1 December 1170. He was received as a hero by the population and this seemed to prove to him that his conduct towards the king had been justified. One of his first acts was to excommunicate all those who had opposed him in his exile and he also renewed the bans of excommunication on the king's advisers and officials.

The excommunicated bishops went to Normandy to lay their complaints before King Henry. Archbishop Roger of York told him, "While Thomas lives you will have no good days, nor quiet times nor a tranquil kingdom." In a fury the king cried out his famous invitation to his knights to settle the matter. "The man Becket ate my bread and mocks my favour," he said. "He tramples on the whole royal family. What a parcel of fools and dastards have I nourished in my house that not one of them will avenge me of this upstart clerk."

With these words the king had sealed Becket's fate. Four knights, Reginald Fitzurse, Hugh de Moreville, William de Tracy and Richard le Breton, left the table and made their way to England.

It would appear that Becket expected and indeed courted martyrdom. As soon as he had reached Canterbury he had said, "One martyr, St Alphege, you have already. Another, if God wills, you will have soon." When he preached his sermon to a large congregation on Christmas Day he said, "I am come to die among you." He must have known that his actions against the king would renew the quarrel and make it so bitter that retribution would follow.

The four knights crossed the Channel, spent the night at Saltwood Castle and then went on to Canterbury where they arrived at noon on 29 December. They announced that they had been sent by the king to arrest Becket and that may well have been their intention at that time. The abbot of St Augustine's Abbey, who was an enemy of Becket, entertained them and, after dinner, they went to see Becket who was working at the Archbishop's Palace. They told him that the bishops must be restored but Becket refused and told them to leave. In a temper they stormed out to get their weapons and armour and Becket was pulled away by his monks into the cathedral where they thought he would be safe.

Armed and wielding swords, the four knights strode into the darkened cathedral calling out for "the traitor". Becket was in a chapel in the north transept. They attempted to arrest him and take him away but the archbishop, a tall, strong man, pushed them away. They came at him again and he threw de Tracy to the ground. At that de Tracy leapt up and struck Becket with his sword. The others joined in and, in a few minutes, the archbishop lay dead on the ground. His last words were: "Willingly I die in the name of Jesus and in defence of the Church." The four knights clattered out of the cathedral and fled.

It was an act which horrified the whole Christian world and Henry was held responsible. Becket was canonized in 1173 and thousands of pilgrims made their way to his tomb at Canterbury Cathedral where countless miracles were said to have been performed.

Henry's plans for dealing with the Church had to be

shelved in the face of this tragedy. He made penance by walking barefoot through the streets of Canterbury to the cathedral and being flogged by the monks at Becket's tomb.

In the following year another fire destroyed the eastern part of the cathedral. Rebuilding was commenced under the direction of the architect William de Sens. He was injured when he fell from the scaffolding and the work was carried on by his assistant, William the Englishman. This gave the monks the opportunity of erecting a better and more impressive shrine for Becket and in 1220, in the presence of Henry III, the body was taken from the crypt to a new shrine in Trinity Chapel.

It was to remain here until the Dissolution of the Monasteries by Henry VIII. By this time it had been enriched by precious stones as many gifts had been made by pilgrims to Canterbury. Richard I had offered thanks there after his imprisonment, Louis VII of France gave jewels to the cathedral after his son had recovered from a dangerous illness, and other kings and princes were frequent visitors to the shrine.

Henry VIII charged the dead archbishop with treason, contumacy and rebellion. The charge was read at the shrine and, as Becket did not appear from his tomb to answer it, he was found guilty. His bones were scattered and the treasure taken away in carts to the royal treasury.

Canterbury Cathedral was to suffer at the hands of the Puritans during the Civil War. Richard Culmer, a fanatical priest from Minster, was responsible for the destruction of much of the magnificent stained glass in the windows. Mounted on a ladder he poked out the glass with a pike.

Canterbury Cathedral has an overall length of 537 feet. The magnificent nave is 187 feet long with a width of 71 feet. The great Bell Harry Tower soars to a height of 235 feet. This tower had been named after Prior Henry of Eastry who presented the original bell. The present bell, recast in 1635, is rung on the death of a member of the royal family or the archbishop.

The north-west transept of the cathedral is now called The Martyrdom. It was here that Becket was murdered and where his body was first entombed. In what is known as Trinity Chapel his shrine was erected and became the focus of pilgrims for more than 300 years. It was in the centre of the chapel covered by a wooden cover which was raised by a pulley from the roof. The ridges in the stone surrounding the shrine, made by the feet of the pilgrims, can still be seen.

On the south side of the chapel is the tomb and gilded effigy of the Black Prince. His helmet, gauntlets and other armour, now frail with age, are preserved in a case but reproductions hang on a beam above. It was at Canterbury that he married Joan, the Fair Maid of Kent. On the opposite side are the tombs of King Henry IV and his second queen, Joan of Navarre.

In the eastern chapel is St Augustine's chair. It is made of Petworth marble and every Archbishop of Canterbury uses it at his enthronement. There is still some evidence of the days when the cathedral was also a monastery in the cloisters which date from the fifteenth century and in the Norman chapter house where the monks met daily to conduct the business of the house. The cathedral library is the oldest established library in the English-speaking world. It has more than 30,000 books and a large collection of manuscripts going back to the eighth century. The building was destroyed in the bombing of 1942 but has been rebuilt in an improved form.

The great Abbey of St Augustine was not so lucky as the cathedral and is now in ruins. It was founded in 598 to house the monks who came over with St Augustine and was set up outside the city walls of Canterbury in accordance with the Roman ordnance that burials could not take place within the walls. It was to become one of the greatest monasteries in Europe. Its abbots had seats in Parliament as a right and the monks claimed to be subject to no-one except the Pope himself. It was also the most important centre of learning in the country. The early archbishops and Saxon kings and queens of Kent were buried there. On the tomb of St Augustine was inscribed, "Here lies St Augstine, a noble and holy patron of the English".

Archbishop Cuthbert was the first to break the tradition of being buried in St Augustine's Abbey and the manner in which it was done illustrates the hostility which existed between the abbey and the cathedral. Cuthbert instructed

the monks of the cathedral that he should be buried there
and not in the abbey. His death was kept secret for three
days and when the monks arrived from the abbey to claim
his body for burial they were told that they were too late.
The archbishop had been buried in the cathedral. Only one
subsequent archbishop, Jaenberht, who had been the abbot
of St Augustine's, was buried there.

The body of St Mildred was brought from Minster and
buried in front of the altar after the Danes had ravaged the
abbey on the Isle of Thanet. Work on a rebuilding of parts
of the abbey was being considered at the time of the Norman
Conquest but the Saxon abbot fled and his place was taken
by Abbot Scotland, a monk from Mont St Michel, "a
dominant ram of his flock".

Scotland and his successor, Guido, practically rebuilt the
abbey. The Normans considered the old Saxon buildings
completely unsuitable and built a new church, towers and
nave. The bodies of the saints and royal personages were
removed to new graves.

With the fame of the shrine of St Thomas Becket
spreading to every corner of the Christian world, Canterbury
Cathedral far outshone St Augustine's Abbey and it did not
attract the riches or the pilgrims who flocked to the rival
establishment. It was surrendered by Abbot John Essex on 30
July 1538. He was the last of the seventy-two abbots who
had ruled over St Augustine's in the 840 years of its existence. The sites of the royal graves were lost but the tomb of
St Augustine was removed to Chilham. It might have made
this pretty village a religious centre but Archbishop Cranmer
found out that it was there and ordered its destruction.

The buildings were pulled down, the lead stripped from
the roof and melted down and the bell tower demolished.
Some of the lead was used to roof over the King's House at
Rochester and some of the stone went to Calais to repair the
fortifications. In a few years most of the buildings were in
ruins. From the materials was erected the King's House, one
of the posting houses along the road from Dover to London
to accommodate distinguished foreign visitors. It was put up
beside the cloisters and seems to have been built on a considerable scale. It incorporated the great hall of the abbot
and his chapel.

Queen Elizabeth, who presented it to Lord Cobham,
stayed there for a fortnight in September 1573. Charles I
spent one night there when he went to Dover to welcome his
queen, Henrietta Maria. Charles II lodged there when he
came back to this country in the Restoration in 1666.

The house soon fell into decay and the property passed
into private hands. It probably suffered its greatest indignity
when it was turned into pleasure gardens similar to Vauxhall
and Ranelagh. In 1836 a Mr Stanmore of the Canterbury
Theatre owned St Augustine's and he was putting on enter-
tainments in the grounds twice a week. The gardens were
"illuminated with nearly two thousand variegated lamps".
Artists from Covent Garden and Drury Lane were engaged
for the concerts and there was dancing "to a full quadrille
band" in the gardens. There were performances of "slack and
tight-rope dancing and gymnastic exercises" and patrons
were promised a display by "Mr Fenwick the celebrated
artist in fireworks". All this was taking place in the grounds
of the abbey founded by St Augustine. The city fathers of
Canterbury, as can be seen in other examples, seemed to care
very little for the history of their city in those days.

Fortunately better times were ahead for the old abbey.
Within its walls was built St Augustine's Missionary College
from which hundreds of missionaries have been despatched
throughout the world. St Augustine's has again become a
centre of learning. The remains of the abbey are now in the
care of the Department of the Environment. Careful excavation has uncovered the foundations of the old monastic
buildings. Two fine gateways remain, the Fyndon Gate built
by Abbot Thomas Fyndon in 1300, and the Cemetery Gate
built by the sacrist Thomas Ickham in 1390.

Not far from St Augustine's Abbey is the oldest parish
church in Britain. The church of St Martin has been in
continuous use since the sixth century when Queen Bertha of
Kent was worshipping in a building previously used by
Roman Christians.

Evidence that there was a Christian community in Canterbury in Roman times came with the discovery of a cache
of silver spoons dating from the year 400. On two of them
was the symbol used by the early Christians, the chi-rho

formed from the first two Greek letters of the word 'Christ'. It is therefore probable that they used the church of St Martin which has Roman brickwork in its walls.

The Venerable Bede in his *Ecclesiastical History of the English People* written in 731 refers to the church of St Martin at Canterbury. "There was in the year 560 a King of the heathen Anglo-Saxons living in Canterbury named Ethelbert," he says.

> He was a king of some note with the title of Bretwalda or ruler over the whole of southern Britain. The Anglo-Saxon people at this time were in many ways a cultural and artistic people and not the ruthless and ignorant warriors of popular imagination. On the Continent the Christian faith was gaining ground rapidly and Ethelbert noted that, among other things, those who had espoused the Christian cause in battle were predominantly successful. Whatever the cause he decided he would enter into an alliance with the Christian King Charibert of Paris.

This alliance was quite clearly a tentative overture to enquire about the Christian faith and its seeming new powers. The usual method of alliance was adopted by Ethelbert asking for the hand of Charibert's daughter Bertha in marriage. Charibert was a man of wild and ruthless habits and on account of his dissolute ways was separated from his wife who had retired to a nunnery at Tours to bring up their daughter Bertha as a Christian. Charibert and his wife agreed to the marriage provided Ethelbert allowed the princess to continue worshipping as a Christian and to make provision for a priest to minister to her. Thus it was that in the year 562 the Princess Bertha arrived in Canterbury to take up residence in the king's palace. There was on the east side of the city a church dedicated to St Martin which had been used by Roman Christians in Britain. To this church the queen, accompanied by Bishop Luidhard, came to worship.

Each day Queen Bertha and her ladies would come from the palace, which stood on the site of the present cathedral, through the Quenin Gate in the city walls to St Martin's Church on the hill. She had been worshipping there for thirty-five years when St Augustine and his monks arrived from Rome to convert the heathen land to Christianity. St Martin's became for a brief period the centre of the Christian religion in England as St Augustine made it his headquarters until he had founded the abbey and cathedral. He used the church for baptisms and it is probable that King Ethelbert was baptized here. There is a Saxon font in the church and there is a tradition that it was made especially for the baptism of King Ethelbert in St Martin's.

Queen Bertha's daughter Ethelburga spread Christianity to the north when she married King Edwin. She took with her the monk Paulinus who became the first Bishop of York.

In the little church of St Martin's the Roman brickwork is easily discernible with Roman tiles evenly laid in courses. A Saxon doorway pierces one wall. The deep Saxon font rests on a base carved from a medieval millstone. This is the spot from which Christianity spread throughout the country.

The Norman castle at Canterbury was one of the first to be built after the Conquest. Many houses were cleared away to provide the space for the erection of this huge square stone keep. It was another castle on the lines of communication which the Normans put up to keep the Saxon population in a state of subjection. Canterbury was always a royal castle. It was built by the king and remained in the king's possession under the command of a constable appointed by and responsible to the king. Built just inside the city walls it commanded the military road from London down to Dover.

Canterbury was immensely strong with thick walls, an inner keep and an outer ward. It was built partly with Roman materials as one can clearly see the red Roman tiles in some of the walls. Work continued on it into the twelfth century and Henry II spent money on it to strengthen its turrets.

Its history is not impressive. When the Dauphin Louis of France was called in by the barons to assist in the war against King John the castle was tamely surrendered to him. In the Wat Tyler rebellion in 1381 it was easily taken and plundered. It was then used as a county gaol. Some of the Protestant martyrs in the reign of Queen Mary were imprisoned here before being led out to the stake.

Its greatest ignominy was to come in the nineteenth century when it was to be used as a coal store for the gas company. The upper storey has now gone but, in the care of the Corporation, the great stone walls clearly indicate what it was in the days of its youth and strength.

Most of the city walls are still standing but of the ancient gates only one, the Westgate, still exists. It has huge twin turrets put up by Archbishop Simon of Sudbury, the archbishop who was caught and executed by Wat Tyler and his rebels. There had been a gate on this site, probably built in Roman times. Through this gate passed at one time or another most of the people famous in the history of this country.

Henry II walked through here barefoot on his way to do penance at the tomb of St Thomas. Richard I passed through *en route* to the Crusades. King John came through to wed Isabel of Angoulême in the cathedral. Chaucer's pilgrims hurried through, "the holy blissful martyr for to seek". The coffins of Henry IV and of the Black Prince were borne through the gate on their way to burial in the cathedral.

Westgate itself was used later mainly as a prison with the guard chambers converted into cells. In the ground-floor chamber, to which the public was admitted, was a circular iron cage. Debtors and other harmless prisoners would be imprisoned here and were allowed to solicit alms and food from the public. Upstairs the dangerous criminals were chained hand and foot to the walls. At the top, over the archway, was the condemned cell from which the prisoner was taken to the gallows in Wincheap Street.

Westgate now has a collection of old arms and armour, special constables' staves, a man-trap and a scold's bridle. The slide for the portcullis and the holes for the chain of the drawbridge can clearly be seen.

It is fortunate that this fine old city gate is still standing as there is yet another instance of the city fathers being negligent of the history of their city. In 1859 Mr Wombwell's menagerie and circus was scheduled to visit Canterbury. Mr Wombwell found that Westgate was too low to allow his elephants to pass through and so he petitioned the Mayor and Corporation of Canterbury to pull it down. One would have thought that such a request would get a sharp rejection but Westgate was very close to destruction. The matter was solemnly debated and then put to the vote. The result was a tie and only the casting vote of the mayor saved Westgate from being pulled down. One can only echo the sentiments of old Walter Jerrold who wrote in his *Highways and Byways of Kent*, published in 1907: "Well might visitors to the city despair of citizens who could turn the ancient abbey into a dancing saloon, could contemplate pulling down an ancient monument for the convenience of a travelling showman or make of a fine Norman keep a coal shed".

As a religious centre Canterbury attracted the friars who believed in taking religion to the people. A party of nine Grey Friars, the Little Brethren of St Francis of Assisi, came to Canterbury in 1224 and were given a site beside the River Stour now known as the Franciscan Gardens. Upon this site they built the Friary church, cloister, refectory, chapter house, library and infirmary. By the rule of their order they could not own property so it was held in trust for them by the City of Canterbury.

The picturesque ruins of their buildings are on show. There is the dorter of the friars, a building raised on arches over the river from which there is a view from the lancet window over the gardens, streams and roofs to the cathedral.

The Grey Friars were followed to Canterbury by the Black Friars of the Order of St Dominic. Headed by Father Gilbert Ash, a party of thirteen Black Friars arrived and presented themselves to Archbishop Stephen. Hearing that they were preachers he ordered Father Gilbert to preach a sermon in one of his churches. The archbishop was so impressed that he favoured their activities and allowed them to found a priory on the river bank in 1236.

Of their buildings the refectory with the barrel-vaulted roof is well worth a visit. It was damaged by bombs in the Second World War but was carefully restored. At the Dissolution of the Monasteries, Blackfriars was converted into a cloth factory but was later used by the Anabaptists and the Unitarians. The building on the west bank which was the infirmary of the friars is once again owned by the Dominican Order.

Christopher Marlowe probably suffered more than most of the famous Canterbury figures during the Second World War. His birthplace was destroyed and St George's Church, where he was baptized, left in ruins.

Marlowe was born in 1564 and in his short life of only twenty-nine years gained a reputation as a playwright. Many people have considered and tried to prove that he was the real author of the plays ascribed to William Shakespeare but without success. They were probably doing Marlowe a disservice for his own plays are good enough to stand on their own.

Marlowe's father was a Canterbury shoemaker who was constantly in debt and often sued for non-payment of bills. Christopher Marlowe was educated at King's School, Canterbury, and at Corpus Christi, Cambridge. He took his degree as Master of Arts and settled in London where he wrote his plays. He was also employed by Walsingham as a secret service agent and it is believed that this work led him to his early death. He was murdered at Deptford in 1593, a murder planned in advance to get rid of a man who knew too much.

He had written by that time some of the greatest dramas in the English language in addition to epic poems. In Canterbury he is commemorated by a bronze figure in the Dane John Gardens. The quatercentenary of his birth was celebrated in 1964 by the unveiling of a plaque on the tower of the ruined St George's Church.

9

Around Canterbury

THE AREA AROUND CANTERBURY is dominated by the Roman roads which run straight down from London, into the city and on to the coast. Some of the villages have now been spared the battery of traffic by having bypasses built round them and have been able to relax again into the slumber of centuries past. Most of the villages in this part of the county are fairly ancient and were there at the time of the Norman Conquest.

In the village of Harbledown, just outside the city where Lanfranc founded a leper hospital, is the Black Prince's Well. It was said to have magical curative powers and many people came from miles to drink the water. The Black Prince was a frequent visitor to Canterbury on his way to take ship at Sandwich and often stopped to drink at the well. When he lay dying in his palace at Kennington, London, he is supposed to have said: "Oh that someone would bring me a drink from the well which is beyond the gate at Canterbury."

The well is enclosed by an arch on which are the Prince of Wales feathers, the badge which the Black Prince took from the King of Bohemia at the Battle of Crécy. The water is now polluted but, up to the beginning of the century, was occasionally bottled and sent to invalids who had written for it.

A few miles away to the west is a turning to the left which leads up to Bigbury Camp. This was the earthwork manned by the Ancient Britons which Caesar stormed when he invaded in 54 B.C. It would appear to have been a massive hill fort but the Romans soon overcame it.

Bigbury is now on private land and so overgrown that it is difficult to make out the lines of defence of this earthwork.

Excavations have shown that it covered 25 acres, measured 1000 feet from east to west and 700 feet from north to south. It had entrances on the eastern and western sides and was protected by a deep ditch. Pottery and metalwork dating from that period have been found together with a slave chain. Possibly the unfortunate slave was glad to see his masters chased away by the Romans but he may have exchanged one form of slavery for another for the Romans took prisoners back to Rome.

Godmersham Park, known and loved by Jane Austen, is a magnificent red-brick mansion on the banks of the River Stour. The area is named after a Saxon thane, Godmar, whose 'ham' or domain it was. It belonged to the Valoign family and, in the reign of Richard II, passed by a queer trick of fate to a family named Austen. It then consisted of separate manors. One of these was taken over by Thomas Scott, a relative of the Earl of Arundel, and he was most annoyed when a family of yeoman stock named Brodnax moved into the other one and styled themselves 'gentlemen'. "They are but parchment gentlemen for their money, of some two or three years antiquity," he said.

In spite of these protests the Brodnax family had come to Godmersham to stay and, in course of time, did become 'gentlemen', In 1727 Thomas Brodnax, who seems to have been extraordinarily fortunate in the matter of wills, inherited some money under the will of Sir Thomas May and, in accordance with the terms, changed his name to May. Only eleven years after this he inherited some more money under the same conditions and again changed his name, this time to Knight. He built the handsome manor at Godmersham Park and, proof that the family had achieved importance in the county, his son Thomas married a daughter of the famous Kentish family, Knatchbull.

At this time a family named Austen was living at Horsmonden. George Austen was educated at Skinners' School, Tonbridge, and at Oxford. He took holy orders in 1760 and Thomas Knight, a distant relative, presented him with the living at Steventon, near Basingstoke in Hampshire. He married Cassandra Leigh, daughter of a Fellow of All Souls, Oxford, and they had eight children. The seventh, a girl, was christened Jane.

One of his sons, Edward, became very friendly with the Knight family at Godmersham and, when Thomas Knight died in 1794, Godmersham Park was left to him. Edward then changed his name to Knight.

Jane Austen and her sister Cassandra were frequent visitors to Godmersham and it was here and at the country houses in the area that she absorbed the atmosphere and studied the characters which she was to portray in her novels. Rather like Charles Dickens, she was adept at studying places and people and registering them in her mind to use at the appropriate time in her books. The mansion at Godmersham Park appears as 'Rosings Park' and Godmersham vicarage is described as the parsonage in *Pride and Prejudice.*

Life at Godmersham is described in the many letters which she wrote from there. In 1808 she was writing to her sister Cassandra, "Yesterday passed quite à la Godmersham. The gentlemen rode about Edward's farm and returned to saunter along to Bentigh with us."

Jane took up the game of battledore and shuttlecock while at Godmersham and seems proud of her prowess. In another letter she says: "Yesterday was a quiet day with us. My noisiest efforts were writing to Frank [brother] and playing battledore and shuttlecock with William [nephew]. He and I have practised together for two mornings and improve a little. We now frequently keep it *three* times and once or twice *six*. We live in the library except at meals and have a fire every evening."

In a later letter she is saying: "We dine at Chilham Castle tomorrow and I expect to find some amusement. I am all alone, Edward gone to the woods. At the present time I have five tables, eight and twenty chairs and two fires all to myself."

Godmersham is open to the public on certain days in the summer.

Chilham is, like Scotney and Sherborne in Dorset, not one castle but two. The old Norman keep stands behind the Jacobean mansion which was erected in the seventeenth century.

Chilham was a hill fort of the Ancient Britons which was

stormed and captured by Caesar's legions. On Juliberry Down, on the opposite bank of the River Stour facing Chilham Castle, is buried a Roman tribune, Quintus Laberias Durus, who was killed in that fight. Roman remains have been found at Chilham suggesting that they built a small fort on the height. Saxon kings including Hengist and Withred lived here but at the time of the Norman Conquest it was owned by Sired, a Saxon thane. Sired fought on the side of Harold at the Battle of Hastings and, in consequence, lost all his lands. Chilham was just one of the estates grabbed by Bishop Odo, Earl of Kent. The estate, which was let out to a Norman named Fulbert de Luxy, was valued at £40.

It was Fulbert de Lucy who built the Norman keep at Chilham. He had been given the property after Odo had been banished for plotting against the king. One of the conditions for holding Chilham was that soldiers should be provided for the garrison at Dover Castle. Under this Fulbert had to provide fifteen knights to do guard duty at Dover for twenty weeks in the year. He built one of the towers at Dover which was named after him and the family then took the name of 'de Dover' instead of 'de Lucy'. This guard duty continued until the reign of Henry III when it was commuted for the payment of a sum of money.

The original castle at Chilham was probably built of wood but this was soon replaced by the great stone octagonal keep which can be seen today. The de Dover family were paying £78 a year in 1202 to the king for the possession of Chilham Castle.

King John paid frequent visits to Chilham for the hunting and hawking and his natural son Richard was married to Roese de Dover, a descendant of Fulbert. They had no children and the estate came into the hands of the Earl of Athol who was executed for treason in 1307.

Bartholomew of Badlesmere, whom we met at Leeds Castle, was granted the estate by Edward II in 1312. He had been a steward at the court but joined the rebel barons in the fight against the king, was captured at Boroughbridge and sent to Canterbury where he was hanged, drawn and quartered.

His son Gyles managed to get the estate back from Edward III but when he died childless Chilham passed to a family named de Ros. This family supported the Lancastrians in the Wars of the Roses and were able to regain Chilham Castle after the Battle of Bosworth when the then Lord de Ros was created Earl of Rutland by Henry VII.

In the next reign Henry VIII gave Chilham to Sir Thomas Cheney, Lord Warden of the Cinque Ports, who pulled down part of the keep, floated the stone down the river and then along to the Isle of Sheppey for the building of his Shurland Castle, which has now vanished. The castle and estate were sold and eventually came into the hands of Sir Dudley Digges who built the present Jacobean mansion. Work was begun in 1603 and not completed until 1616. Sir Dudley became Master of the Rolls and, on his death, left an annuity to be given as prize money for races between the men and women of Old Wives Lees and Chilham every year on 19 May. These races continued right up to the reign of Queen Victoria.

Subsequent owners enlarged the park and laid out the splendid gardens. A fine cricket ground was made and in 1878 the first Australian team to visit the country played a match at Chilham. There is a picture in the National Library of Australia which shows this match being played with the Norman keep and the Jacobean mansion in the background. The great Australian batsman, Charles Bannerman, was in the team as was Spofforth, the demon bowler. The Chilham side included Lord Harris who was to captain Kent for many years.

Chilham is now owned by the thirteenth Viscount Massereene and Ferrard whose peerage dates back to Charles II. It is open on certain days of the year.

Over the entrance to the mansion is an inscription put up by Sir Dudley Digges – "The Lord is my house of defence and my castle". During excavations in the old Norman keep the dungeons were discovered and in there were fifteen skeletons. The gardens were laid out by Capability Brown and include an evergreen oak reputed to have been planted in 1616 to mark the completion of the mansion. Some of the mulberry trees are more than 500 years old. Cuttings from these were taken by a member of the Digges family who became the first Governor-General of Virginia. He took them over to America and planted them on an island which has since been known as Mulberry Island.

Displays of falconry are given in the grounds which now also house the Battle of Britain museum with relics of the planes which fought in the Second World War.

The abbey built by King Stephen at Faversham was enormous. The church was more than 300 feet long. It was founded as a Cluniac monastery in 1147 but became a Benedictine house in later years. While it was being built Queen Maud stayed at Canterbury to keep an eye on the progress. The abbey was dedicated to St Saviour.

Queen Maud was buried there in 1152, Prince Eustace (their son) in 1153 and King Stephen himself in 1154. As a royal abbey it flourished and many gifts were made to it. As was the case with other monasteries the rule became lax and archbishops made adverse reports on their visitations. A porter was summarily dismissed for "causing the access of dishonourable women into the building after nightfall". In 1533 Abbot John Sheppey complained that "rooks, crows, choughs and buzzards are stealing the fruit" and asked for a licence to shoot "these said ravenous fowls". There are still plenty of rooks and crows in the county but it is many years since choughs and buzzards have been seen in Kent.

Henry VIII made one visit to the abbey before it was dissolved on 8 July 1538. The buildings were pulled down and what was left was given to Sir Thomas Cheney, Lord Warden of the Cinque Ports. Queen Mary and her husband, King Philip, paid a visit but any ideas she had of restoring it had to be abandoned for decay had set in. Other visits were made by Queen Elizabeth and Charles II but Faversham's only other connection with royalty was when James II was kept there for a short period after being captured by Faversham fishermen when he was attempting to escape to France.

By 1671 the church had gone but the refectory was intact and was being used as a store. The gateways and porter's lodge were still standing but had gone by 1774. All that now remains of this once great royal abbey is a stone wall incorporated into the side of a house. There is no trace of the royal tombs and the land on which the great church stood is now used as playing fields.

The oldest gunpowder works in this country were at Faversham. They were in operation certainly by 1558 and continued up to 1934 when they were closed.

Gunpowder was manufactured before this in Europe and for many years England was forced to import supplies. Firearms and cannon were used in the Wars of the Roses but the primitive weapons of those days often did more harm to the user than to the enemy.

In time of war the foreign supplies of gunpowder might be cut off and so it was essential to establish a home-based industry. There were a number of conditions to be met by the site chosen for the works and Faversham was ideally suited for this purpose.

First there was the question of the supply of the raw materials for the manufacture of gunpowder – charcoal, saltpetre and sulphur. The sulphur and saltpetre were imported and therefore the site would have to be near a seaport. As the English army and navy was based in the south, this seaport would also have to be in this area to cut down the cost of transport. Charcoal, made from charred wood, would require a large quantity of timber and therefore there should be wooded country behind the seaport. Again Faversham was ideally suited.

Another requisite was a water supply to drive the water mills which would provide the power for the factory and also provide the safe means of transport between the various works where the powder was made.

Faversham was a seaport with a stream, situated between London and the Channel ports, with the Kentish woods just behind the town to provide the charcoal.

The first recorded owner of the Faversham gunpowder works was Daniel Judd who was apparently a Parliamentarian who had become wealthy as a result of sequestering Royalists' estates in the Civil War. When the war broke out with the Dutch in 1652 production of gunpowder had to be increased. The Admiralty asked Judd to step up the output at Faversham and he installed an extra mill. He guaranteed an annual supply of 100 tons of gunpowder and it was not long before 2 tons of gunpowder were being shipped each week up the Thames to the Tower of London which was used as a store.

Judd's methods did not find favour with the Faversham Borough Council who complained that he had tampered with the watercourse and converted a flour mill into a gunpowder magazine. He was threatened with legal action but the Government stepped in to inform the Council that Judd had been authorized to use the flour mill to step up production of gunpowder. The Borough Council had to withdraw and allow Judd to continue.

Later on in 1742 when the works were owned by a family named Grueber the Borough Council brought in a bylaw to prevent loose gunpowder being taken through the town in open carts with a fine of 40 shillings for each offence. An Act of Parliament in 1771 gave more general powers to the authorities in the carriage of gunpowder.

The mills were being expanded and improvements were stepped up when the works were taken over by the Government in 1760 and became the Royal Gunpowder Factory administered by the Board of Ordnance. By 1774 output had been stepped up to 364 tons a year.

Precautions against the effects of an explosion included the building of tall, thick screens and the planting of trees around the plant which could absorb the blast. These were to be tested in April 1781 when three tons of gunpowder exploded. Three men were killed and the explosion was heard up to 50 miles away. A pillar of flame shot up, houses were destroyed or damaged and streets were blocked. Damage was estimated at £1,500.

Following this disaster the more dangerous processes were transferred to another site away from the town. A new set of safety regulations was drawn up under which workmen had to wear slippers inside the works to prevent sparks being struck off shoes with nails, the hinges of doors and windows oiled to prevent friction and barrels of gunpowder brushed with a soft brush to remove all grit.

By the end of the eighteenth century Faversham was employing a work force of 400 and turning out nearly 600 tons of gunpowder a year. This was needed by the armies engaged in the war against Napoleon, but at the end of that war the Government disposed of the works.

The factory was owned by John Hall and Son but production fell as demand for gunpowder was reduced. With the invention of guncotton, claimed to be six times as powerful as gunpowder, the new owners built a guncotton factory, the first in the world. Shortly after they had started production in 1847 there was an explosion in which twenty people were killed. Two buildings blew up, houses were damaged, trees torn up by the roots and a field of wheat blasted and ruined. The guncotton factory was immediately closed and production ceased.

By 1914 Faversham was also making TNT in addition to other explosives and this was responsible for the worst disaster in the history of Faversham. On 2 April 1916 some empty bags caught fire and these set fire to a TNT store which contained 80 tons of explosive. Attempts were made to put out the fire but the store suddenly exploded. More than 100 people were killed. Of these, seventy were buried in a mass grave at the Borough Cemetery.

After that war the works were gradually closed down and gunpowder production at Faversham finally ceased after 370 years. In 1969 the Faversham Society started to restore the old Chart Mills to preserve the features of what was once the most flourishing industry in the town. These mills are open to the public on certain days in the year.

The little village of Fordwich on the River Stour three miles from Canterbury has a population of 150 but in the Middle Ages it was a prosperous port and a member of the powerful Cinque Ports Confederation. This membership entailed the provision of men, ships or money in time of war but also meant the allocation of valuable privileges in return.

The river was navigable from Sandwich up as far as Fordwich which was then used as the port for Canterbury. This brought prosperity to Fordwich in the shape of dues paid at the quays. The monastery of St Augustine at Canterbury held the land at Fordwich and, under an edict of Edward the Confessor, was given the Saxon power of 'sac and soc', the power to judge criminal and civil cases.

The monopoly at the Fordwich quays enjoyed by St Augustine's led to an acrimonious dispute with the rival establishment of Christ Church, Canterbury, which was then engaged on improvements to the cathedral. Stone and lead were being imported from France and landed at Fordwich for which dues had to be paid to St Augustine's. In order to cut down the costs, the prior of Christ Church, who owned an adjacent riverside site, built his own quay and a storehouse. The incensed abbot of St Augustine's ordered these to be demolished. The prior put them up again and they were promptly pulled down. This dispute was only settled when another landowner offered Christ Church the free use of his own quay.

Fordwich had become a corporation somewhere about 1240 and was governed by a mayor and twelve jurats. They were elected in the parish church by the whole community and still retained their right to try criminal and civil cases. The mayor also acted as coroner but did not seem to relish this duty for there is one recorded case in which he instructed the town sergeant to put a corpse into the river and let it float down the river to Sandwich.

The income for the small town came mainly from dues on the quays and this source of revenue was jealously guarded. When a barge-owner decided to go further up the river to land his goods at Canterbury the men of Fordwich blocked the river and seized his barges. Eventually, with the coming of the railway, this water-borne traffic died out and this spelled the end of prosperity for Fordwich.

Membership of the Cinque Ports had been kept up and the mayor, two jurats, a freeman and the town sergeant never failed to attend the Cinque Ports Courts of Shepway and Guestling. This continued up to 1861 when no representative turned up at the Court of Guestling. The clerk called three times in succession but, as no-one answered, the membership of Fordwich was severed.

Fordwich was also famous for its salmon-trout in the river. These were netted every night during the fishing season which lasted from April to October. The netted fish were handed over to whoever owned the 'turn' for that night and participation in these 'turns' was a highly-prized privilege. Among those to whom these were allotted were the Mayor of Fordwich, Lord Camden, the Lord Warden of the Cinque Ports, the Earl of Winchelsea, the Archbishop of Canterbury, the Mayor of Sandwich and the Town Clerk of Fordwich. In 1744 the Town Clerk was in bad odour with the corporation and it was solemnly decreed that "he shall have no more turns in the water".

The Court Hall, which dates from the twelfth century, is still there and can be seen. It is certainly the smallest in the county for it measures only 31 feet by 23 feet and had to accommodate the mayor, twelve jurats, the town sergeant, freemen, and any other interested parties. As there was no heating it was the custom to hold winter meetings in the public house opposite. The jury room is only 8 feet by 8 feet giving the twelve members of the jury only 5 square feet of floor space each. Also to be seen are the prison cell, the stocks and the ducking-stool.

The Fordwich Corporation lasted, rather surprisingly, until 1876 when, after a report by a Royal Commission, it was disbanded.

South of Canterbury, on the Dover road, is Broome Park, now a hotel. The house was one of the first to be built in this country of English bonded brick. Dating from 1635, it was erected by Sir Basil Dixwell, a Warwickshire squire who had inherited land in the Folkestone and Canterbury area. It was at this period that brick was becoming popular for building and Broome with its high Jacobean gables was in advance of architectural design at that time.

Broome is connected with one world-famous figure, Field-Marshal Lord Kitchener of Khartoum who bought the property for £14,000 in 1911. It then consisted of the house and 500 acres and in the following year Kitchener purchased an adjoining 50 acres for another £1,000. He planned to spend his retirement from the army partly at Broome and partly in East Africa. He had purchased an estate in Kenya and it was his stated objective to spend the summers at Broome and go to Kenya for the winters. He was never to fulfil this dream.

As soon as he had bought Broome he gutted the interior and filled it with the treasures which he had collected from all parts of the world during his army career. Kitchener loved Broome and spent as much time as he could on the estate effecting improvements. He personally designed the fountains with nymphs and sea monsters in front of the rose garden. He had been known as a great collector and was not apparently too scrupulous in his methods. If he wanted

The magnificent gateway of Eastwell Park near Ashford

The tomb of Richard Plantagenet in the church at Eastwell Park

Lympne Castle near Hythe

Canterbury Cathedral

Below: The ruins of St Augustine's Abbey, Canterbury

St Martin's Church, Canterbury

The ruined Norman keep of Canterbury Castle

Godmersham Park near Ashford, where Jane Austen stayed

Chilham Castle, near Canterbury

The old Court House at Fordwich near Canterbury

Broome Park, near Canterbury, former home of Lord Kitchener

The towers of the Saxon church at Reculver

The walls of the Roman castle at Richborough

The Viking ship at Pegwell Bay, Ramsgate

Bleak House, Broadstairs, former home of Charles Dickens

A sign on a house at Broadstairs whose owner refutes any claim to a Dickens connection

The 'Ham Sandwich' signpost near Deal

Kingsgate Castle near Broadstairs

The chequered Barbican Gate at Sandwich

The ancient Fisher Gate on the quay at Sandwich

Dover Castle, "the key to the gateway of England"

Below: The Roman Pharos at Dover Castle

St Radegund's Abbey near Dover

Saltwood Castle near Hythe. *Above:* The great gatehouse

Below: The courtyard and well

Deal Castle, erected by Henry VIII

Walmer Castle, residence of the Lord Warden of the Cinque Ports

A martello tower at Dymchurch

The Royal Military Canal at Hythe

something he said so and in this fashion was the recipient of a number of gifts which the donor felt forced to yield up to the great soldier. During the First World War when Kitchener was Secretary of State for War he was making a tour of the battlefields in Belgium. In Ypres he inspected a group of statues which had survived the bombardment of the German artillery. Noticing Kitchener's keen interest in the statues, a staff officer remarked, "These statues have been bombarded by the Germans for 100 days but they have never been in so much danger as they are today. They will be pulled down and erected in Broome Park before this war is over."

Kitchener spent his last hours in England working in the garden at Broome. He left on 3 June 1916 for Scapa Flow to embark in the cruiser *Hampshire* which was to take him to Russia. The *Hampshire* struck a mine shortly after leaving Scapa Flow and was sunk. Kitchener was drowned.

Although it is now more than sixty years since Kitchener left Broome, he is still remembered there. The double entwined 'K's' (Kitchener of Khartoum) are still on the walls, and over the fireplaces, carved in large capitals, in his motto – "Thorough".

10

The Isle of Thanet

THE ISLE OF THANET is no longer an island for the Wantsum, the deep channel which separated it from the rest of Kent, is now silted up and reduced to a drainage ditch over much of its course. The Wantsum was an important waterway in the time of the Romans and was guarded by forts at each end. It saved the haul round North Foreland for shipping coming from up the English Channel and into the Thames for London.

The Romans built four forts or castles in Kent to guard their harbours. Reculver (Regulbium) was at the northern end of the Wantsum with Richborough (Rutupiae) at the southern end. At Dover (Dubris) the fort has entirely disappeared and there are now only scattered remains of Stutfall Castle at Lympne (Portus Lemanis).

These square forts had perimeter walls 12 feet thick and 30 feet high enclosing an area of 6 or 7 acres. They had towers at the corners and at intervals along the walls and four main gates. Most were built in the third century when Saxon pirates were raiding Britain and were placed under the command of the Roman official whose duty it was to repel them – the Count of the Saxon Shore (*Comes Litoris Saxonicum per Brittanicum*). He had his headquarters at Richborough from where he commanded the nine forts which stretched from Brancaster in Norfolk to Portchester in Hampshire.

Thanet is now a holiday area dominated by the great seaside resorts of Margate and Ramsgate. It was a Margate man, Benjamin Beale, who invented the bathing machine which was a feature of seaside resorts up to the Second World War. He was a Quaker and introduced his bathing machines at the start of the eighteenth century when sea bathing had been recommended by doctors and was then becoming popular. Beale's bathing machines were drawn down to the water by horses and had large awnings which could be pulled down so that the bather entered the sea unobserved. A piece of advice pinned up in one machine read:

Let me say to the parties who take this machine,
Don't stay in the sea till you turn blue and green.

Probably the proprietor was anxious that his customers did not keep the machine too long and prevent him from hiring it out to others. There seems to have been plenty of customers who had to wait their turn for a machine. At Margate waiting rooms were provided "fitted up with every luxury including newspapers and a piano with a rich banjo tune".

Beale's bathing machines spread to every seaside resort in the country and lasted for more than 200 years.

More than half of the Roman fort at Reculver has now been washed away by the sea and most of the Saxon church built on the site was torn down by its vicar. It is probable that the Romans put up a small fort here soon after their invasion of A.D. 43 but the main fort was built about A.D. 210.

It was a square fort protected by two ditches with walls 600 feet long and covering an area of 8 acres. In design it was similar to the forts built at the same time on Hadrian's Wall. From the top of the wall the sentries could see far out to sea, watch for shipping using the Wantsum and the approaches from the land. It had four gates and the road from Canterbury came straight in at the west gate. Within the fort was the headquarters building measuring 140 feet by 110 feet, one of the largest of its type. This contained the sacellum, the sacred shrine where the regimental standards were kept. Evidence of the date of the building of Reculver has come with the finding of a tablet inscribed "For the Emperor. Fortinatus built this shrine of the Headquarters with the cross-hall under Aulus Triarius Rufinus consular governor". Fortinatus was in command of the unit which built the fort at the time when Aulus Triarius Rufinus became consular governor in Britain in A.D. 210. Other buildings within the fort included the barracks for the troops, bath houses and store-room.

In the fourth century Reculver was garrisoned by the First Cohort of Baetasians, numbering about 600 men. Roman bricks bearing the regimental stamp of this unit have been found. This cohort originally came from Brabant in Belgium. They were one of the first to serve in Britain and had seen action in Scotland and in Cumberland.

After the Romans left Britain, Reculver was deserted but the site was soon taken over by missionaries from Rome who had followed in the wake of St Augustine. In 669 Egbert, King of Kent, founded a monastery on the site. Material from the Roman walls was used to build the church which was originally only 37 feet long but was enlarged in the twelfth century. As with other monastic houses near the Kent coast it suffered badly during the raids by Danish pirates and had to be abandoned for a period.

Under the Normans, Reculver became a large and rich church with two great towers and a village had grown up around it. Its greatest enemy was the sea which, over the centuries, was pounding the coast and carrying away the walls of the old Roman fort year by year. As if this attack by the elements was not enough, this fine old Saxon church was then attacked by its own vicar. The young Rev. Nailor, newly appointed to Reculver in 1806, decided that the church was unsuitable and bullied his parishioners into agreeing to pulling it down and using the material to build another and more convenient church inland. The parish clerk recorded the last service in Reculver church as "The last text that Mr Nailor took was 'Let your ways be the ways of righteousness and your path the path of peace' and down came the church and what was his thoughts about his flock that day no-one knows."

Fortunately Trinity House, which had for years used the twin towers of Reculver as a landmark for mariners, stepped in and saved what was left. Groynes were erected on the shore to keep back the encroaching sea and the ancient towers strengthened. They are still used by mariners today.

The old monastery possessed two great treasures which disappeared. One was a great gospel book in uncial letters and the other a 9-foot high ancient stone cross. The book disappeared in the Reformation and the cross was broken up at the same time.

The mighty walls of Richborough Castle overlooking Pegwell Bay remind us that for hundreds of years this was the real Gateway to Britain, long before Dover took that title. It was here that the Romans landed in A.D. 43 and it was their principal port during their years of occupation. Richborough Castle can claim to be, with Hadrian's Wall, the most important Roman building in this country. Guarding the southern entrance of the Wantsum, it was once the symbol of Rome's might and power.

As soon as they had established themselves in Britain the Romans built up Richborough as their main port and supply base. Store rooms and granaries were erected and through the port came the legions who were to carry the Roman law throughout the country and up into Scotland.

In A.D. 85 they erected a huge building cased in marble with bronze statues to commemorate the final conquest of the island by Agricola and in honour of the Emperor Domitian. Although later destroyed, the foundations of this monument still exist. It was in the form of a cross and towered above the fort. The natives and new arrivals coming over in the ships up the Wantsum would see this as evidence of the might of the Roman Empire and it must have been an impressive sight, rising out of the heart of the fort and dominating the landscape.

Richborough was the headquarters of the Count of the Saxon Shore and was always well garrisoned. For some time the famous Second (Augusta) Legion, with which Vespasian conquered the south and west of England, was stationed here, although its main base was at Caerleon in Monmouthshire. Richborough had good communications with other Roman forts and towns and is, in fact, the start of the famous Watling Street which leaves by the west gate, on to Canterbury and London and then north to Chester.

Richborough was a square fort like the others around the coast with walls 600 feet long but the whole of the eastern wall has now disappeared. It had the usual four gates with towers at intervals. The walls, 13 feet thick, rose to a height of 30 feet and from these the Roman sentries could see along the Wantsum to Reculver and out to sea. There were the usual barracks and stores and the remains of a wine cellar have been discovered with the conical holes in which the wine jars were stored. The grave of a Roman soldier, who was buried with his shield, sword and spear, was found beside the walls.

When excavated, Richborough yielded up a vast amount of Roman remains. These included a pig of lead inscribed with the name of the Emperor Nerva, a bust of the Empress Faustina, and toilet articles such as mirrors, combs, glass phials for cosmetics, manicure sets and tweezers and an article described as an ear-scoop. The military equipment included spears, swords and daggers and caltrops, spiked objects thrown on to the ground to injure and impede cavalry. More than 50,000 coins covering the 400 years of Roman occupation came to light together with some Saxon silver pennies of the reigns of Offa and Canute.

To while away the long periods off duty the Romans played games which required gaming boards, dice and bone counters. Some of the pieces of pottery which have been dug up bear the names of the makers. Many tiles were stamped by the tiler Silvius and some show the imprints made by hob-nailed boots and the paws of dogs and other animals. Most of these fascinating items are housed in a museum on the site.

After the legions left Britain the Saxons moved in and occupied the fort. At some time a chapel, dedicated to St Augustine, was built beside the east wall and it was here that the Saxon coins were found.

St Augustine is said to have landed at Richborough and in former times pilgrims were shown a stone on to which he stepped on landing which retained the print of his foot. Lambarde does not seem to have heard of this for he would have had some scathing comments to make. Another theory is that St Augustine landed a few miles further north at Ebbsfleet on Pegwell Bay where a Celtic Cross was erected by Lord Granville in 1884.

Ebbsfleet was the landing place of Hengist and Horsa in 449. To commemorate the 1,500th anniversary of this landing an exact replica of their longship was rowed over to

Ebbsfleet in 1949. This Viking ship, *Hugin* with a dragon's head and lined with shields can be seen at this site.

Minster Abbey goes back to Saxon times. The manor here was held by Egbert, King of Kent. The heirs to the king were his two nephews and it was suggested to him by one of his thanes, Thunnor, that these boys would try to oust him from the throne when they grew up. Better to kill them now, said Thunnor, and offered to do the deed. The king agreed but repented afterwards and went to the archbishop to ask how he could make recompense for the murders. The archbishop ordered him to found an abbey for the boys' sister, Domneva, who had taken a vow of chastity. Egbert agreed and asked Domneva how much land she would need. "I will need as much land as my hind can run over in one run," she replied.

The hind was let loose but Thunnor rode across its path to scare it off. Then, says the legend, the earth opened up and swallowed the thane. A pit on the hill above the village is supposed to be the place and is known as 'Thunnor's Leap'.

Domneva built her abbey at Minster and handed it over to her daughter, Mildred. She remained the abbess for the next thirty years and the community prospered so much that a new monastery and church were built. Mildred, who had been canonized, was buried in the new building.

During the rule of the fifth abbess, Seledritha, the Danes had started their raids on the coast of Kent. They burnt down the abbey and the nuns perished in the flames. The tomb of St Mildred, buried beneath the ground, survived.

The site was abandoned but, 200 years later, it was given to the monks of St Augustine's at Canterbury. In spite of local opposition, the remains of St Mildred were taken to Canterbury for burial.

The monastery was rebuilt as a lodge for the monks but eventually came into the possession of the Conyngham family who held it from 1680 down to 1928. In 1937 it was purchased and given over to Benedictine nuns who still occupy the site. The ruins are open for inspection and visitors can see the cloisters, the site of St Mildred's tomb and the ruins of the church.

Broadstairs is Charles Dickens territory and is proud of it. It stages a Dickens festival each year at which the local residents dress up as characters from the novels, hold readings from his works and attend lectures by members of the Dickens Fellowship. Even outside this festival it is difficult to get away from Dickens in Broadstairs. Restaurants and bars bear the names of his characters, there is a Dickens Museum, and houses in which the novelist stayed are proudly pointed out. Indeed one resident has gone one better than this by placing a sign on his house, "Charles Dickens did not live here".

Broadstairs was a favourite holiday resort with Charles Dickens and he paid many visits to the town. He went there in 1837 and stayed in a house in the High Street where he finished writing *Pickwick Papers* and started *Oliver Twist*. In 1839 he was back again to a house in Albion Street (now a hotel) where he wrote *Nicholas Nickleby*. He took a fancy to a house on the cliff overlooking the harbour, previously occupied by another author, Wilkie Collins, then known as Fort House from its grim crenellated aspect. He eventually managed to buy it and spent much time there writing *David Copperfield* and other novels. The house was later named Bleak House but the novel of that name was not written there.

Bleak House still has the study in which Dickens worked, his chair and other mementoes.

A few miles up the coast on the edge of the cliff stands a magnificent castle – or so it appears at first glance. Kingsgate Castle is, however, one of a series of follies put up in the area from 1760 onwards by Lord Holland, father of Charles James Fox.

Kingsgate was originally St Bartholomew's Gate but, after Charles II and his brother James had put in there for shelter when their yacht struck bad weather, it was renamed. Lord Holland bought a house on the cliffs there and completely transformed the place. He was stated to be the most hated man in the country for he had been Paymaster General to the Forces during the Seven Years War and had made his fortune. Accused of being a "public defaulter of unaccounted millions" he decided to retire from public life and to live in Thanet for his health.

His first building, which still stands, was Holland House which overlooks the bay. It was built in the style of an Italian villa and he filled it with antiques from Egypt, Italy, Greece and other Mediterranean countries. In the grounds he put up mock ruins. His stables were built to resemble a castle and this, added to by later owners, is the magnificent structure which crowns the cliff today. It has square towers, a curtain wall and a massive turreted gateway. Guest rooms were built in the style of a convent with cloisters and cells and a 'ruined' chapel. This has now become a school and the castle converted into flats.

A Bede House was built on the opposite cliff. Part of this fell into the sea but the remainder was incorporated into a public house, the Captain Digby. This Captain Robert Digby was a drinking companion of Lord Holland who left a sum of money in his will so that Captain Digby's health should be drunk in the inn on his birthday "as long as the noble Bob shall breathe".

Other follies put up by Lord Holland in the area included towers to Neptune, to Thomas Harley (Lord Mayor of London in 1768), to Margaret, Countess of Hillsborough, and to Robert Whitfield from whom he bought the property. Only the last now survives.

Probably the only piece of genuine history at Kingsgate is the two tumuli with graves and urns on the site of a battle fought between Saxons and Danes. Lord Holland opened these up in 1765 and promptly erected a monument with an inscription:

> To the memory of the Danes and Saxons who were fighting for the possession of Britain (soldiers think everything is their own), the Britons having been perfidiously and cruelly expelled. This was erected by Henry, Lord Holland. No history records who was the commander of this action or what was the event of it. It happened about the year 800 and that it happened on this spot is probable from the many bodies which are buried in this and the adjacent tumulus.

Most of Lord Holland's follies have now disappeared but they must have given him and other people a great deal of fun in their time.

To the north of Thanet near Margate is Salmestone Grange, an ancient Benedictine monastery which contains important buildings which have been restored. It formerly belonged to the nuns at Minster Abbey but, when that abbey was burned by the Danes, it was given to St Augustine's at Canterbury. There was a dispute over the ownership of Salmestone and its 40 acres in 1194 and the case was decided in the King's Court at Canterbury. The monks were confirmed in possession in return for a small annual rental.

Salmestone and its monks were under siege in 1318 when there were riots in Thanet. A great deal of damage was done to the monastery and the rioters were fined £600 to pay for repairs, a very heavy sum of money in those times.

As with other religious houses, the monks were expelled in 1538 and the buildings passed through the hands of a number of owners before they were bought and then presented to the Abbot and Community of the Benedictine Abbey at Ramsgate.

The medieval buildings, although altered and restored, are almost complete. They include the monks' refectory built in 1320, the chapel dating from 1326, the guest rooms, monastic kitchen and the dormitory. Pieces of the ancient altar were found but the holy-water stoup near the door of the chapel is the original one used by the monks. Although broken into pieces, it was still in perfect condition and reassembled.

Parts of Salmestone have now been converted into flats but there is enough left to convey a very clear idea of life in the days when it was a Benedictine monastery.

Near by is Quex Park, named after a family called Queke who had held it in medieval times. This family line ended with a daughter in the sixteenth century who married Henry Crispe, a sheriff of Kent, who became known as 'King of the Isle of Thanet'. One of his descendants, Sir Henry Crispe, was the victim of an audacious kidnapping during the Commonwealth. A Royalist, "dashing Captain Golding" with a party of forty men, came over from Flanders and landed at Birchington. Armed with carbines, pistols, swords and poleaxes they went to Quex Park, broke down the door, plundered the house and carried off Sir Henry to Bruges where he was held against a ransom of £3,000.

The family applied to Oliver Cromwell to sanction to raise the ransom money but Cromwell, suspecting that it was a trick to raise money for Charles II in exile, refused. Crispe remained a captive in Bruges for eight months before a portion of the estate was sold to raise the ransom money. The only word of French which he had picked up during his captivity was *Bonjour*. He used this repeatedly on his return and was known to the villagers as Bonjour Crispe.

William III and Queen Mary were frequent visitors to Quex Park where the king would await a favourable wind to take him to Holland. There are two towers in the park. One was built by the owner, an enthusiastic bell-ringer, in 1819 to house a peal of twelve bells and to celebrate the victory at Waterloo. The other was intended for celebratory cannon fire.

At Quex Park is the Powell-Cotton Museum which contains the zoological exhibits of the later Major Powell-Cotton who apparently spent all his life shooting animals and sending them back to Quex Park. His exhibits are splendidly displayed but was it really necessary to kill so many wild animals? One gets a rather guilty feeling from the sad eyes of row upon row of these beautiful creatures gazing down reproachfully upon the visitor.

11

The Invasion Coast

THE COAST OF KENT is within sight of the cliffs of France and the short sea crossing has naturally attracted the invader. Romans, Saxons, Jutes and Danes landed in Kent and, although William the Conqueror went to Pevensey in Sussex, he quickly moved in to subdue Kent after the Battle of Hastings. The Spanish Armada, Napoleon and Hitler all planned to invade Britain through landings in Kent. The county has therefore had to look to its defences and these included, as the headquarters of the Cinque Ports Confederation, the provision of warships for the king.

The first invasion came before anyone had thought of repelling it at sea and the Romans sailed unmolested from Boulogne across the Dover Strait in 55 B.C.

Julius Caesar describes this landing in his commentaries. His fleet reached Britain about 9 a.m.

I saw the enemy forces standing under arms all along the heights. At this point of the coast precipitous cliffs tower over the water making it possible to fire from above directly on to the beaches. It was clearly no place to attempt a landing so we rode at anchor until about 3.30 p.m. awaiting the rest of the fleet. . . . After moving about 8 miles up channel the ships were grounded on an open and evenly shelving beach. The natives, however, realized our intention. Their cavalry and war chariots were sent ahead while the main body followed close behind and stood ready to prevent our landing. Disembarkation was an extraordinarily difficult business. On account of their large draught the ships could not be beached except in deep water and the troops, besides being ignorant of the locality, had their arms full. Weighted with a mass of heavy armour, they had to jump from the ships, stand firm in the surf and fight at the same time. But the enemy knew their ground. Being quite unencumbered, they could hurl their weapons boldly from dry land or shallow water and gallop their horses which were trained to this kind of work. Our men were terrified. They were inexperienced in this kind of fighting and lacked that dash and drive that always characterized their land battles.

Caesar describes how he manoeuvred his ship to bring on a flank attack on the Britons who were "scared by the strange forms of the warships, the motion of the oars and by the artillery which they had never seen before".

But our men still hesitated mainly because of the deep water. At this critical moment the standard-bearer of the Tenth Legion, after calling on the gods to bless the legion through his act, shouted "Come on, men. I, at any rate, shall do my duty to my country and my commander." He threw himself into the sea and started forward with the eagle. The rest were not going to disgrace themselves. Cheering wildly they leapt down and when the men in the next ship saw them they too quickly followed their example.

Caesar says that the action was bitterly contested but, when everyone was ashore and formed up, the legions charged and the enemy was hurled back.

In the following year, 54 B.C., he came back and landed unopposed.

Some prisoners revealed that a large native force had originally concentrated on the beaches but had withdrawn and hidden themselves at Bigbury Woods when they saw the numbers of our fleet . . . Troops of the Seventh Legion, working under cover of interlocked shields, piled up lumber against the fortifications, stormed the position and drove them from these woods at the cost of only a few minor casualties.

Caesar's invasions were only raids and he soon went back to Gaul. The island was to be left in peace for the next ninety years but when the Romans returned they stayed for 400 years and completely transformed the country.

The Cinque Ports stretch along the Kent coast and into Sussex. There are actually seven and not five for Rye and Winchelsea were added to the original ports of Sandwich,

Dover, Hythe, Romney and Hastings. Of these seven, only Dover is now a port. The sea is now a long way from Sandwich, Romney, Rye and Winchelsea. Hastings and Hythe, although on the sea, no longer have harbours.

In medieval times the Confederation of the Cinque Ports was a very powerful body, responsible for the defence of the coast and of the Channel crossing. They started in the reign of Edward the Confessor but did not receive a royal charter until 1278. The ports were made responsible for supplying ships and seamen for the service of the king which made them, in effect, the navy of the country. In return for this they were allowed many privileges. They were freed from taxes and tolls, had the right to judge thieves, possession of any wrecks in their area and also 'den and strond' at Yarmouth. This right to 'den and strond' was very important in those days for the men of the Cinque Ports could land at Yarmouth to dry their nets and sell their fish at the Yarmouth Herring Fair. This led to hostility between the Cinque Ports and Yarmouth and there were a number of battles between them. The worst was in 1297 when Edward I called out the fleet to attack the French. They were sailing into battle when the ships of the Cinque Ports spotted some from Yarmouth. They quickly forgot about the French fleet and turned on the Yarmouth ships. In the fight thirty-two Yarmouth ships were destroyed and 200 men killed.

The Cinque Ports had their own courts of Shepway and Guestling which adjudicated on matters affecting the Confederation. The Court of Shepway still meets today but only for the installation of a new Lord Warden.

The barons of the Cinque Ports also had one honour which they greatly cherished – the right to bear the canopy over the head of the king or queen at the coronation procession and seats at the right hand of the monarch at the banquet. There was trouble over this at the coronation of Charles II when the king's footmen tried to take the canopy from them. The barons won the struggle but by that time had lost their places at the top table. There was another scuffle at the coronation of George IV but, although the barons were again victorious, this was the last coronation at which the canopy was carried. They still retain, however, the right to places of honour at the coronation.

The silting up of their harbours and the foundation of the Royal Navy marked the end of the power of the Confederation of the Cinque Ports.

The treacherous Goodwin Sands lie about four miles from the coast and have been the graveyard of many a fine ship. They were once a fertile island, part of the territory of the father of King Harold, Earl Godwin, after whom they were named. When the tide goes out the sands harden and it is possible to walk on them. A number of games of cricket have even been played there. When the tide comes in they vanish beneath the waves and any ship which becomes stuck on them is gradually sucked under.

There is a legend that the Goodwins were once protected by a sea wall. It fell into decay and stone was sent to repair it but this stone never reached the Goodwins. It was taken by the local vicar and used to build the steeple of Tenterden church. Unprotected, the Goodwins sank beneath the sea to become the menace to shipping which they are today. And so, says the legend, Tenterden church is to blame for the loss of ships on the Goodwin Sands.

Only 21 miles separate the Kent coast from that of France and these waters were the scene of great activity in the last two wars. The Dover Patrol was set up in 1914 to keep the seas safe for the millions of men who crossed and recrossed the Dover Strait to the battlefields of Flanders. Day and night, the convoys were guarded by warships from Dover Harbour. There was also a net barrage from coast to coast to prevent German submarines from slipping down the English Channel. This was guarded by armed trawlers and lit by flares at night. There was a fierce naval engagement in 1917 when two German destroyers were sunk but the enemy was more successful in 1918 when their ships dashed out and sank eight of the trawlers guarding the net barrage.

During that war the Dover Patrol had been responsible for guarding 125,000 ship passages through and across the Dover Strait and had lost seventy-three ships. An obelisk to the memory of the men of the Dover Patrol stands on the white cliffs above St Margarets.

The Dunkirk evacuation was organized from Dover when,

in six eventful days, 316,000 men were rescued from the beaches and brought safely home. In that operation the 220 naval vessels were assisted by an armada of 660 small craft which included lifeboats, yachts, paddle steamers and motor launches.

The great days of Sandwich as one of the most important ports of the country are long since past. But, in spite of the lorries which rush through its narrow streets, it retains the air of a medieval town. Quaint old buildings lean towards each other across the cobbled streets and the medieval quays are still in use.

It was the chief harbour for the export of wool and Edward I ruled that this was the most important product to go through the port. Being near to Canterbury, most of the important travellers came this way. Archbishop Thomas Becket fled from the wrath of Henry II through Sandwich and came back to face his martyrdom. Richard I, released from prison, came through Sandwich on his way to Canterbury to give thanks for his deliverance. Edward III, the Black Prince and Henry V embarked from here for their wars in France and the pretender, Perkin Warbeck, was beaten back by the local men when he tried to invade.

The town suffered a great disaster in 1457 when the French raided the port. The mayor was murdered, houses burnt and goods carried off. To this day the mayor of Sandwich wears a black robe in mourning for his dead predecessor.

An even greater disaster befell Sandwich when the Wantsum began to silt up and render it no longer usable as a port. By the middle of the sixteenth century the harbour was blocked and the only access to the sea was by the narrow, winding River Stour. The city fathers realized that this would spell the end of prosperity for the town and sought assistance. They invited Queen Elizabeth to pay a visit and had high hopes that she would put work in hand to restore the port.

They took great pains over this visit. The streets were cleaned and repaved, buildings repaired, pigs banned from the town and butchers ordered to dump their offal outside the gates instead of leaving it in the road. The streets were strewn with rushes and sweet-smelling herbs and houses decorated with flags and flowers.

The queen came in from the direction of Deal to be greeted with a salute from the cannon. She was entertained to a mock battle and a fight between two men in boats who, with staves, attempted to push the other into the water. Both fell in and the queen was highly amused.

The party sat down to a feast in the schoolhouse at which no fewer than 160 dishes were served. As a parting gift, Sandwich presented her with a gold cup worth £100.

As the royal party went on their way there was much optimism in Sandwich that steps would be taken to clear the port and restore it to its former position. Unfortunately the queen did nothing and Sandwich was left to survey its silted-up port and to lament the vast amount of money, including the £100 for the gold cup, which had been spent on the royal visit. The final blow came when a ship sank at the entrance to the harbour and could not be moved. The sand soon covered it and spelled the end for Sandwich as a great port.

The Barbican, dating from the sixteenth century, now controls a toll bridge which replaced the original drawbridge. It has colourful chequered towers to the north side facing the river. Another of the old gates facing on to the quay, the Fisher Gate, also stands as it did when Becket walked through it.

Sandwich has suffered much in the past from raiders from the sea and from the sand which silted up its harbour. Now its enemies are the lorries which shake the ancient houses to their foundations as they rumble past.

Dover Castle, described as "the key to the gateway of England", has been a fortified stronghold from the days of the Ancient Britons right up to 1958. The Romans, although using Richborough as their main port, recognized the importance of Dover and erected the pharos or lighthouse on Castle Hill on the seaward side of the mighty Norman keep. There was another on the cliffs at Boulogne to guide the Roman galleys across the short sea passage.

The Dover Pharos rises in five stages, the top stage being added in medieval times. The four lower stages are built of flint and rubble, octagonal in plan enclosing a chamber 14 feet square. At the top a fire was kept burning at night so that the flames could be seen far out to sea.

The town of Dover suffered severely from bombing and shelling in the Second World War but this had one beneficial result for archaeologists in that Roman remains came to light. There was a small Roman town here with substantial stone buildings and, at that time, Dover was a small port concerned, as it is today, with the cross-channel traffic. It was also one of the bases for the Roman fleet and also one of the forts controlled by the Count of the Saxon Shore, although all traces of this fort have vanished.

Evidence that such a fort existed comes in a document of Saxon times when, around A.D. 640, Eadbald, King of Kent, founded a monastery "within the castle". It is clear that the Roman fort at Dover, like that of Reculver, was used by the early Christians. Of this church the only remaining relic was a tombstone of a Saxon named Gisheard with a cross and a Runic inscription.

Later, probably in the reign of King Canute, a Saxon church, St Mary-in-the-Castle, was erected at the side of the Roman Pharos. This is still intact, although much restored and reconstructed in the last century. Its stone walls include reused Roman bricks obviously taken from the Roman fort.

There was certainly a castle on the hill by the time of the Norman Conquest. Eadmer, a monk of Canterbury, relates the history of Harold's visit to William at his court in Normandy. During that visit, Harold swore on holy relics to support William for the crown of England on the death of Edward the Confessor and also to build a castle at Dover. By 1066 this castle had been built and contained the wall which is on the south side of the church. After the Battle of Hastings William marched into Dover but the castle held out against him for a time. It eventually fell to the Normans and the governor, Bertram de Ashburnham, and his son were executed. Dover Castle was then placed in the hands of Odo, Earl of Kent, the step-brother of the Conqueror. Its first constable was John de Fiennes who had the assistance of eight Norman knights to command the garrison.

The castle was soon tested when Eustace of Boulogne was called in to support Kentish Saxons in a revolt in 1074 which was speedily crushed. The castle was under siege but held out. Odo himself was the next to stage a rebellion against William II but again Dover Castle remained intact. It was then taken over by the Crown and has remained a royal castle ever since. Henry II was responsible for the entire rebuilding of the castle. He raised the great keep, built the inner ward, and replaced the defences of the outer ward with strong stone walls. Between 1168 and 1174 he spent £325 on Dover Castle, a sum equivalent to £50,000 today. A few years later another £1,100 was spent on the keep and the curtain walls and Henry had made Dover one of the strongest castles in the world at that time. There were twenty-seven towers around the outer wall and fourteen along the inner ward.

Dover Castle was severely tested in the civil war which broke out in the reign of King John. The castle was then held by one of the greatest soldiers of the day, Hubert de Burgh, and he resolved to hold it for the king. The barons brought over Louis, the Dauphin of France, and offered him the crown of England. Although John was soon dead the fight continued against his son, Henry III. The French forces soon had control of the coast but Dover Castle held out against them. Louis called on Hubert to surrender and sent two English barons to discuss terms. One of them was Hubert's brother, Thomas, who had been captured and was sent to the castle loaded down with chains. The herald sounded his trumpet and, accompanied by five archers, Hubert came to the battlements. His brother called on him to surrender as, if the castle had to be taken by storm, the garrison would be massacred and Hubert himself hung from the top of the 83 foot high keep. If Hubert would surrender the castle Louis would give him the counties of Suffolk and Norfolk. "Get you gone, you traitors," replied Hubert. "One more word and I'll command my archers to shoot you down."

Louis brought up his siege artillery and laid siege to the castle from June to December. Although hard-pressed and reduced in numbers, the garrison held out, refusing more calls to surrender. The nearest the French came to success was when they blew in the northern gate with a mine but Hubert and the garrison blocked up the entrance with timber. Relief came when Sir Stephen de Pencestre brought up a force of 400 bowmen who crept up from the cliffs and entered via the sally port. Louis was then forced to call off the siege.

It would be thought that Hubert de Burgh would have been held in high regard by the king for his loyal defence of Dover Castle but the fickle Henry III found fault with him soon afterwards. Hubert was imprisoned, chained to the wall of Devizes Castle and robbed of his possessions. Eventually he was restored to favour, then disgraced again and was forced to flee to sanctuary. It was certainly a sorry fate for the loyal hero of the long siege of Dover Castle.

Sir Stephen de Pencestre became Constable of Dover Castle and the statutes for the garrison which he promulgated have survived and throw light on life in the castle in those days.

The gates were shut at sunset and twenty warders stood guard on the castle walls. Any warder found outside the walls was placed in the dungeon prison and "punished in body and goods". If the chief warder found a warder asleep, "he shall take something from him as he lies or carry away his staff or cut a piece out of his clothes to witness against him". If, out of pity, the chief warder failed in this duty he would be sentenced to prison "dur en fort", taken to the gate of the castle and expelled, and he would also lose all his goods found within the castle walls. For striking another warder with the flat of his hand a warder could be fined 5s, with the fist it was increased to 10s. and for wounding it went up to 15s. The light in the church was to be kept burning and the priests were ordered to pray "for the recovery of the Holy Land, the success of Christianity, the King, the Royal Family, the Barons of the Realm, the Constable and all the garrison".

Another statute ordered that

If the King arrives unexpectedly in the night the gates shall not be opened to him, but he shall go to the postern called the King's Gate toward the north and there the Constable and those who accompany him may admit the King and a certain number of his suite. When the King is admitted he has the command and in the morning, when it is full day, he may admit the remainder of the company.

As the kings of those days travelled with a large retinue there would have been possibly more than 100 of his attendants left shivering outside the walls if the king arrived at night. Dover Castle appears to have become a favourite residence for the start of the married life of kings and queens. Edward II came here with his bride Isabelle and stayed for two days. Richard II first met his bride, Anne of Bohemia, at the castle, and later Charles I received Henrietta Maria of France at Dover where the royal apartments were fitted out at great expense. James II also met his bride, Mary of Modena, at the castle.

Henry VIII was often at Dover Castle when supervising the building of his coastal castles against the threat of war by the Catholic powers. He and Katherine of Aragon stayed here while on their way to the Field of the Cloth of Gold.

A beautifully engraved cannon, 24 feet long, near the Canon's Gate is known as Queen Elizabeth's Pocket Pistol and is claimed to be able to throw a 12-pound ball up to a distance of 7 miles. Queen Elizabeth visited Dover during her tour of Kent and this cannon probably commemorates her visit. On this occasion she was given a great welcome by the townsfolk and the mayor was prepared with a long address of welcome. The queen had heard many of these during her tour and was probably heartily bored by the length of them. The mayor, a short man, climbed on to a stool and started: "Most gracious queen, welcome..." He was not allowed to get farther than this for the queen cut him short with: "Most gracious fool, get off that stool!"

In the Civil War the Parliamentarians obtained control of Dover Castle "by subterfuge and cunning infiltration". The Royalists attempted to regain control but, after an ineffective bombardment, were driven off by a relieving force.

During the Napoleonic War the towers of the inner ward built by Henry II were levelled off and filled with rubble to make gun platforms, heavy cannon brought in and repairs made to the defences.

Dover Castle is now in the care of the Department of the Environment and open to the public. It stands on the top of the famous white cliffs, symbolic of the defiance of the nation at every threat of invasion during the past 900 years.

On the hills behind Dover are the remains of St Radegund's Abbey. It was founded in 1192 as a house of the Premonstratensians, the white canons, one of the two English abbeys colonized direct from Prémontré. The abbey was in difficulties from its early days and there was a proposal to move it to River but in 1210 it was properly established. A large church 183 feet by 98 feet and a cloister 70 feet square were built. Under a grant from Richard I the canons added 100 acres to the estate.

St Radegund's always regarded itself as superior to the other Premonstratensian house, Bayham Abbey in Sussex, and on one occasion demonstrated this in what can only be called an act of highway robbery. One of the canons from Bayham was on his way back to there from Canterbury when he was held up on the road at Ash by canons from St Radegund's. They took from him his horse, prayer book and a purse containing 48 shillings. The Abbot of Bayham charged Abbot William of St Radegund's with robbery but was calmly told that it was in accordance with a mandate from the parent house of Prémontré. The Bayham canon was rebellious and did not pay proper respect to St Radegund's and was therefore punished in accordance with the mandate.

Bayham was not satisfied with this and brought a lawsuit against St Radegund's. Surprisingly the jurors found for St Radegund's which reinforced the statement of that house that it was superior to Bayham.

In the later years of St Radegund's there were many complaints about the conduct of the canons. They were accused of going out and absenting themselves for long periods and gambling with dice and cards.

In 1500 Abbot John Newton was charged with frequenting taverns and using bad language but managed to hang on to his position.

In 1536 the abbey was suppressed and the stone used for building the Henry VIII castles on the Kent coast. What was left was bought by Simon Edolph who made a house out of the refectory and turned the tower of the church into a gatehouse.

There are still important ivy-clad remains to be seen. These include the gatehouse, part of the nave of the church, the transept, chapter house, cellar and the refectory.

St Radegund's superiority over Bayham, the cause of their quarrel, can be said to have been maintained into the twentieth century for the remains of St Radegund's are more extensive than those of Bayham.

The impressive castle of Saltwood now lies behind Hythe, three miles from the sea, but in Roman times the sea flowed up to the foot of the bluff on which the castle stands. The forest came down to the shore and, as the trees were often under water, the name of Saltwood was given to the district.

The first castle on this site was built by Oisc, King of Kent, who succeeded his father Hengist in 488. Saltwood is shown on a charter of King Egbert in 833 and in 1026 a deed signed by King Canute and Earl Godwin assigned the castle to the cathedral church of Canterbury.

In Domesday Book of 1080 Saltwood is shown as being held by Hugo de Montfort who carried out some extensive repairs. His grandson, Robert de Montfort, supported the wrong side when Robert, eldest son of William the Conqueror, unsuccessfully challenged Henry I for the crown, and was forced into exile. All his estates were forfeited to the crown.

In the reign of King Stephen, Saltwood was held by Henry d'Essex, Constable of England and Standard Bearer to the king. He came to a sad and humiliating end for the holder of such high offices. During the fighting on the Welsh border in 1163, d'Essex rode into an ambush. He flung away the king's standard and took to his heels. When he reached camp and the story got around he was accused of cowardice by a Robert de Montfort, a descendant of the earlier holders of Saltwood. The two men fought a duel and d'Essex was left lying wounded on the field. He was cared for by monks who nursed him back to health and he joined them in their monastery.

Thomas Becket, Archbishop of Canterbury, then laid claim to Saltwood Castle as one of the estates belonging to the Church. He described it as "the most pleasant house in Kent". This was at the period of the quarrel between the king and the archbishop and, to spite him, Henry II presented Saltwood to Sir Ranulf de Broc, a fiery baron who was one of Becket's sworn enemies. De Broc moved in with a large garrison and turned the castle "into a den of thieves".

When Henry made his famous outburst against the archbishop the four knights left Normandy and travelled to Kent. They stayed overnight at Saltwood with de Broc and it was here that they plotted the murder of Becket. They set off for Canterbury on the following morning with an escort of cavalry provided by de Broc.

Saltwood Castle remained the property of the Crown until the reign of King John when it was restored to the diocese of Canterbury. A royal visitor who enjoyed the archbishop's hospitality was Edward II.

Another visitor who certainly did not enjoy the hospitality of Saltwood was the Lollard William Thorpe, who was imprisoned on the ground floor of the castle for sixteen years. He had been found guilty of heresy after publishing "A Short Testament to his faith" and was lucky to escape the stake. The tower in which he was incarcerated is still known as the Thorpe Tower. In 1380 an earthquake damaged Saltwood Castle and he managed to escape.

In 1381 Saltwood Castle acquired a real friend when Archbishop William Courtenay inherited the estate. He was archbishop for fifteen years and during this period spent vast sums on improvements to the castle and park. Courtenay sold other church property to raise the money. The keep was enlarged, two huge watchtowers erected and the rooms for the clergy on the south side of the inner bailey were improved. The height of the watchtowers was governed by the need for the sentry to command the old Pilgrim's Road from the coast to Canterbury.

Saltwood Castle remained in the possession of the archbishops until the reign of Henry VIII when Archbishop Cranmer "observing the murmurs and envy that his possession of this and other sumptuous houses brought on him found himself obliged to part with it and in 1540 conveyed the castle back to the crown". Henry promptly gave it to Thomas Cromwell but, when he was beheaded, it went back into royal hands. Edward VI presented it to John Dudley, Earl of Warwick, but he exchanged it for other property and Lord Colinton obtained it.

In the reign of Queen Elizabeth it would appear that Sir Walter Raleigh stayed at Saltwood for there is an item in the accounts: "10d for the shoeing of Sir Walter Raleigh's horse".

Saltwood Castle then passed through the hands of many owners, none of whom appear to have taken much care of the place. Stone was stolen from the crumbling walls and huts were put up to house livestock which were then kept in the bailey to protect them from poachers. The Deedes family from Goodnestone acquired Saltwood in 1794 and, during the course of their ownership which was to last until 1925, undertook some restoration.

Saltwood was sold by auction on 23 September 1925 and was then bought by Mr R. L. Lawson whose widow married the great castle enthusiast, Lord Conway of Allington. She employed the distinguished medieval architect Sir Philip Tilden to restore Saltwood to some part of its former glory.

For more than fifteen years a team of masons was employed cutting and matching the stones to the original design. This continued until the outbreak of the Second World War brought this work to an end. The last major project, the restoration of the barbican and its ruined arches, had to be left uncompleted.

Lady Conway died in 1953 and Saltwood Castle was bought by Lord Clark, famous for his great 'Civilisation' series on television. He had his study in the great hall of the castle and when he moved out in 1970 it was taken over by his son, Alan Clark, M.P. for the Sutton Division of Plymouth.

Further work of restoration, including excavation of ground not previously dug, is now planned.

Saltwood Castle is now open on certain days during the year. Visitors can see the Roman tower, the 60-foot deep well which connects with a stream which runs under the castle, and go up on to the battlement walk formerly patrolled by the sentries. At the foot of Thorpe's Tower is an ancient yew tree said to have been planted by Richard II.

From the battlements can be seen the Secret Garden. In the torture chamber there are a set of stocks and other implements.

The grounds are beautifully maintained and enhanced by the presence of peacocks which stroll grandly among the old walls.

12

The Castles Built by Henry VIII

THE WARS OF THE ROSES virtually destroyed the old nobility and the Tudors were able to bring an era of comparative peace and security. Castles were no longer needed as fortified residences and, in any case, the strong Tudor monarchs would not have allowed them to be built.

The external policy of the country during the reign of Henry VII and the early years of Henry VIII gave little cause for alarm. The attempt to reconquer the former territories in France was abandoned and Tudor statesmen pursued the policy of the Balance of Power to give England security against the great continental powers.

All this changed with the Reformation which was really responsible for ushering in the next great age of castle building. The Pope, outraged by England's defection from the Catholic Church, called for a war which would bring the heretic nation back to the true faith. His first task was to reconcile France and Spain and when these countries agreed to a truce in 1538 the Pope launched his crusade to re-establish his authority which Henry had destroyed in the Reformation.

England now faced invasion by a Catholic power and had to defend its coastline. The State embarked on a system of coastal defences and, true to the Tudor system of government, Henry undertook this work himself. A chain of castles from Yorkshire to South Wales was built but the largest and most important were those in Kent "which keep the Downs" – the stretch of water between the Goodwin Sands and the coast.

Four castles were built on the Kentish coastline within a distance of 16 miles from Deal to Folkestone. These were at

Sandown, Deal, Walmer and Sandgate. Blockhouses mounting cannon were built along the Thames at Gravesend and Milton and also at Dover but of these only the Moates Bulwark below Dover Castle remains. The castle at Queenborough built by Edward III was inspected and hurriedly repaired and given modern armament.

Henry's castles on the Kent coast are low squat buildings with thick rounded walls designed to deflect cannon balls. They were probably designed by a Bohemian engineer named Von Haschenperg who was at that time employed by the government. Guns were mounted in tiers on platforms to cover every approach and, in addition to the gun ports, there were embrasures for small arms.

These castles were immensely strong but were never put to the test as the threatened invasion did not take place. Neither were they troubled in Elizabeth's reign for the Spanish Armada was routed before it came within reach of the coast. In fact only one shot was ever fired from these castles. This was in June 1628, nearly 100 years after they had been built, when "the Admiral of a fleet of Hollanders having passed Walmer Castle without striking his flag was fired into as he passed Deal Castle and was made to haul down his colours". They did, however, see some fighting during the Civil War.

In 1642 the four castles were taken over by the parliamentary forces without any opposition and everything remained quiet and peaceable until the Kentish Rising in 1648. More than 10,000 Men of Kent and Kentish Men took up arms and declared for the king and the Royalists quickly captured the four Henry VIII castles on the coast. The rebellion was to be short-lived and a parliamentary army moved into Kent to regain the county for Cromwell. The castles were besieged and Sandgate fell. The Royalists successfully raised the sieges of Deal and Sandown Castles by landing troops from the sea but were beaten off at Walmer and the castle surrendered.

The Parliamentarians renewed their efforts at Deal and Sandown. Attempts were again made by the royalist fleet to relieve them from the sea, aided by sallies by the garrisons, but were again beaten off. A contemporary account by a parliament commander says:

The enemy sallied out to Deal Castle and intended to surprise our forlorn guard which was between three and four hundred yards of the castle but they were soon discovered and were gallantly repulsed and driven back to the very gates of the Castle and this with the loss of three of our men and some few wounded. As for the loss on the Enemies' part it is not certain, yet some of our Souldiers observed about eight or nine of them to be carried off on pick-pack.

The strongest attempt came in August when the Royalists landed 800 troops from the sea. There was heavy fighting on the shore but the Royalists were repulsed with losses of 80 killed and more than 100 taken prisoner, including their commander Major-General Gibson. The parliamentary forces lost only seven men. Shortly after this, Deal and Sandown Castles were captured. Their garrisons still had plenty of provisions and arms but realized that the chances of relief attempts were almost hopeless. The castles had seen the last of active warfare.

Running from north to south, Sandown at the end of the promenade at Deal is the first we reach. Only the site now remains but the outline gives some idea of its size, strength and position. As with the other three castles, Henry VIII was able to save money in building materials by using stone taken from the nearby Kentish monasteries which had been suppressed. Some of the stone for Sandown Castle came from the Carmelite monastery at Sandwich. This monastic Caen stone at Sandown misled one amateur archaeologist in the last century into the 'discovery' of a Norman monastery there until it was pointed out that Henry VIII had used the monastic stone to build his castles.

Sandown was completed in 1540 and, like the others, placed under the control of the Lord Warden of the Cinque Ports. It had a garrison of eighteen under a captain who was paid £30 a year. It was a quatrefoil castle, shaped rather like a four-leafed clover, measuring 165 feet by 165 feet with walls 14 feet thick. It had a circular tower in the centre with the guns mounted there and on the lower outer bastions. Although maintaining a garrison of various sizes, little was done to keep it in repair after the Civil War. It was described then, after its surrender to the parliamentary commander,

Colonel Nathaniel Rich, as "much battered after last summer's leaguer".

With the restoration Sandown was used as a prison for the regicide, Colonel John Hutchinson. He had made submission to Charles II but was arrested and imprisoned in Sandown in 1664. His wife unsuccessfully petitioned the king to share his imprisonment but this was refused and, to be near her husband, she took lodgings in what she described as "the cut-throat town of Deal". She visited him daily at the castle where he occupied himself by sorting and classifying sea-shells until his death four months later.

High seas and tides battered the castle walls and Sandown was sold and demolished in 1863. Some of the stone was used for the repair of Walmer Castle. Another lot went to Eastry to build a chapel at the Union. It is not known if any of the Caen stone from the monasteries was included in this but if so this stone would then have returned to its original religious use.

Next along the coast is Deal, the largest of the castles, standing on the shore in the middle of the town. This is a sexfoil castle 234 feet by 216 feet. It also has walls 14 feet thick with 145 embrasures for firearms. Surrounded by a moat, the castle has a central circular keep with an outer curtain. Six semi-circular bastions project from the keep and the outer curtain also has six matching bastions, one of which is the gatehouse. There are embrasures for guns in the parapet of the keep, and in the parapets of the inner and outer bastions. Deal has five tiers of gunports facing in all directions which make it an immensely strong castle.

The gatehouse had a drawbridge and portcullis with murder holes in the roof through which defenders could assail any attackers who had reached the door. In the walls of the entrance hall can be seen the Caen stone from the dismantled monasteries. The inner doorway opens outwards and this was designed to prevent anyone who had gained the entrance hall from blocking the doors and using it as a stronghold. With the door opening outwards it could not easily be secured from the inside.

The keep has a central spiral staircase and some of its gunports have now been converted into windows. This was the living quarters of a garrison of twenty-four commanded by a captain. The basement was used as a storeroom, the ground floor had a kitchen and the soldiers' accommodation and the captain's quarters were on the first floor. At the top of a keep is a lantern.

The garrison was increased and extra stores put in at the time of the Spanish Armada but after this scare was over a period of neglect set in. By 1615 a report made on the castle stated that it was in a dangerous condition, the sea-wall was eaten away and the lantern decayed. It was estimated that the cost of repairs would be nearly £400, and of this £240 would have to be spent on a jetty to keep back the sea. In spite of numerous complaints no work was done and in 1634 the estimated cost had risen to £1,200. Repairs were then undertaken and these must have been effective as they enabled Deal to withstand the sieges during the Civil War.

It was estimated by Colonel Rich that £500 would have to be spent to repair the damage which his troops had inflicted on the castle. It continued to be garrisoned and kept in a state of readiness during the Dutch wars. After this various alterations were made to improve the accommodation and amenities for the captain. During the last war a German bomb fell on the castle and destroyed these later additions and so it can now be seen almost as it appeared when first built by Henry VIII. It is owned and maintained by the State and open to the public.

Walmer Castle has a picturesque setting amongst the trees and behind a huge shingle bank which has been piled up by the tides. This is another quatrefoil castle 167 feet by 167 feet with the same design of a circular central keep and four bastions. The central spiral staircase has now been replaced. The basement was the storehouse but the two floors above, which were the living quarters of the captain and the garrison, have been extensively altered. It is surrounded by a dry moat. The gatehouse is in one of the four bastions and originally had a drawbridge and portcullis with the usual murder holes over the entrance. It had four tiers of gunports, three in the bastions and the other on the top of the keep. Each bastion had seven gunports with another in the wall between the bastions. Its original garrison comprised a captain and seventeen men. The guns used at that time were similar to those which can still be seen at Walmer although these date from the Napoleonic Wars. In all there were sixty gunports covering all angles. These guns had an effective range of up to two miles.

Walmer, like its neighbouring castles, was never tested in Tudor times and by 1616 needed repairs to keep out the sea. Estimates for repairs rose steadily year by year until by 1634 nearly £1,500 was required. At that time a sea wall costing £600 was built and further repairs were put in hand.

Walmer also suffered in the sieges of the Civil War and needed another £300 to be spent on it to make good the damage. It continued to be garrisoned over the years but in 1708 it became the official residence of the Lord Warden of the Cinque Ports. Extensive alterations have been made since to make it suitable for residence but these do not detract from the original design of the fabric to any great extent. The gatehouse was heightened, staircases inserted in place of the central spiral staircase, and the rooms panelled.

Many famous statesmen have occupied the office of Lord Warden. William Pitt lived at Walmer from where he supervised the building of the martello towers to defend the coast against Napoleon's army. His niece, the eccentric Lady Hester Stanhope, stayed at Walmer and planned the beautiful gardens which stretch beyond the walls.

The Duke of Wellington made it his home for twenty-three years and it was here that he died. His writing-desk and iron bedstead are still in the castle and another room has been converted into a museum containing objects associated with the duke. He entertained Queen Victoria and the Prince Consort at Walmer in 1842 and the rooms and furniture they used can still be seen.

Another holder of the office was Mr W. H. Smith, of bookstall fame, a First Lord of the Admiralty and the original 'Sir Joseph Porter' satirized in the Gilbert and Sullivan opera *H.M.S. Pinafore*. He was mainly responsible for collecting and preserving the pictures and prints in the castle.

W. H. Smith wanted to become a clergyman but was persuaded to join his father's news agency business. It was his enterprise that led to the establishment of W. H. Smith bookstalls on every railway station and the business flourished. When Smith became interested in politics he was a Liberal, but when his application for membership of the Reform Club was rejected he became a Conservative. He entered Parliament in 1868 and became Secretary to the Treasury in Disraeli's Government of 1874. In 1877 he became First Lord of the Admiralty where he was rated a successful minister. Later appointments included Secretary of State for War and Leader of the House of Commons.

Smith was Lord Warden for only six months and died in office at Walmer Castle on 6 October 1891.

Sir Winston Churchill was Lord Warden for twenty-four years and, although he did not reside at the castle, always flew the Lord Warden's standard on the bonnet of his car.

Sir Robert Menzies, the present Lord Warden, was appointed in 1965. A former Prime Minister of Australia, he is a popular figure in Kent where he is a freeman of Sandwich and of Deal. His love of cricket and his contribution to the game were recognized when he was appointed president of the M.C.C. in 1962 and of Kent County Cricket Club in 1969. It is noteworthy, in the cricket context, that Sir Robert was born in Melbourne on 20 December 1894 at the exact time that the England team scored an 'impossible' victory over the Australians at Sydney. The Australians had scored 586 in their first innings, a world record at that time, and forced England to follow on. No test match had been won by a team following on but this was the exception as England won by a few runs as Mrs Menzies proudly nursed her newly-born son who was to grow up to become such an enthusiast for the game.

Walmer Castle is owned and maintained by the State and can be visited at any time except when the Lord Warden is in residence.

The most southerly of the Henry VIII castles is at Sandgate between Folkestone and Hythe. It was in trefoil design and measured 200 feet by 150 feet and 650 feet in circumference. It was built in three tiers with the usual central keep and three bastions. On the landward side was the gatehouse with drawbridge and portcullis. The gun platform facing the sea was 100 feet long and mounted eight cannon. The garrison consisted of a captain and thirty-four men.

The complete accounts for the building of Sandgate Castle, which are in the British Museum, show that it was started in 1539 and completed in eighteen months. Stone was quarried locally but Henry VIII obtained most of his building material from Kent monasteries which had been suppressed.

From St Radegund's Priory came 237 tons of stone, from Monks Horton 90 tons and another 32 tons came from Christ Church, Canterbury. In addition to this the contractors supplied 147,000 bricks and 44,000 tiles. The total cost was over £5,000, a staggering sum at that time. Henry took a keen interest in the work, taking "very laborious and painful journeys towards the sea coasts". He visited Sandgate in 1539 and again in 1542 when the work had been completed.

Queen Elizabeth also visited the castle in August 1573 and a room there was afterwards known as the Queen's Chamber. It had earlier housed one of the queen's prisoners, Thomas Keys, her Sergeant Porter who had secretly married Lady Mary Grey, youngest sister of Lady Jane, the ten-day queen who had claimed the throne on the death of Edward VI. Lady Mary was kept at court where Queen Elizabeth could keep an eye on her but managed to get married without the queen's permission. Although Keys held an important position as Sergeant Porter his rank was much inferior to that of the queen's kinswoman. He was arrested, imprisoned and later transferred to Sandgate Castle. From here he petitioned the queen for his release but this was refused and he died in the castle.

By 1616 Sandgate was being badly damaged by the sea and repairs were estimated at £260. This had risen to £560 by 1623 and to £610 by 1635. Repairs were effected in time for it to face the sieges of the Civil War.

During the Napoleonic Wars it suffered drastic alterations which almost reduced it to the status of a martello tower. The outer walls were lowered, the uppermost storey of the central keep removed, the ditch was filled in, the drawbridge destroyed and the surrounding buildings were swept away. After the war was over only two guns remained and the garrison was reduced to five. At one time it was being used as the military prison for Shorncliffe Camp.

The sea was, however, its greatest enemy. The walls had begun to give way and in 1875 the castle was flooded by a high tide. It was abandoned in 1881 and sold. It is now privately owned.

These were the last of the traditional castles to be built in Kent.

13

Romney Marsh – The Fifth Continent

THERE USED TO BE A SAYING in this area that there are five continents in the world – Europe, Asia, Africa, America and Romney Marsh. This is the triangular area reclaimed from the sea bounded by the hills to the north and the coast on the other two sides of the triangle. It is certainly different from other parts of Kent.

Romney Marsh was under the sea in Roman times but it now has some of the finest grazing land for the famous Romney Marsh sheep. The marsh is criss-crossed by dykes and ditches and much of it is below sea-level. Only the Dymchurch Wall prevents the sea coming back over the land.

The Dymchurch Wall is therefore very important and magistrates on the Marsh were once sworn to "Fear God, Honour the King and Maintain the Wall". On the shore are miles of golden sands and it was therefore chosen as a landing place for the projected invasions of Napoleon and Hitler. Its loneliness also made it a favourite area for smugglers.

When Napoleon assembled his army on the cliffs of Boulogne and announced his intention of invading England, defensive measures were put in hand. His plan was to land his army from 2,200 flat-bottomed boats on the coast between Dover and Hastings. He was so confident of success that he had a medal struck bearing the words "Descente en Angleterre" and this was even marked "Struck in London 1804".

To prevent a landing the government erected forts on the shore. These were the martello towers which can be seen at Folkestone, Hythe and Dymchurch. There were twenty-seven in all on the Kent coast and eleven of these are still standing.

The suggestion for these forts came from Captain Ford of the Royal Engineers who had been impressed by the resistance put up by a fort on Mortella Point in Corsica. It took two days of bombardment and assault to subdue it and Captain Ford noted down the details of its plan and construction. When the war with France was renewed in 1803 and an invasion was threatened it was decided to build a chain of these forts which, by that time, had been called martello towers. The building began in 1805 and took two years to complete but by that time the Battle of Trafalgar had been fought and, without command of the sea, Napoleon had abandoned his invasion plans. Nevertheless the building went on and seventy-three martello towers had been completed by 1808.

The martello towers look rather like upturned flowerpots. They were built of brick with cement facings. Most are 33 feet high with the entrance doorway 20 feet from the ground and reached by a ladder which could be drawn up inside. The walls are 13 feet thick at the bottom tapering to 6 feet at the top and some were surrounded by a moat. The door and windows faced inland as they were designed to engage ships at sea and to prevent an enemy landing on the beach.

The ground floor was used as a store, the garrison lived on the first floor and on the flat roof was the gun platform. The armament was an 18-pounder gun and two carronades which could traverse the full circle. These guns could fire round shot, case or grape.

The martello towers were certainly strong and would have stood up to heavy bombardment. When one was tested by having cannon balls fired at it from various ranges, the shot just bounced off the rounded walls. In 1960 a martello tower near Dymchurch was removed to allow the coast road to be straightened. It successfully resisted all attempts to pull it down and eventually it had to be blown up by explosives.

After the Napoleonic War they were put to various uses. They were used as stations by the early coastguards, and others were let out to farmers. One martello tower on the seafront at Hythe has been converted into a fine dwelling house with the thick walls making it cool in summer and warm in winter.

During the Second World War they were again manned

by troops and Home Guards. One tower at Dymchurch has been restored to its original state and is open to the public during the summer. The others still stand facing the sea as a reminder of the days when mothers frightened their naughty children by saying, "If you don't be good, Boney will come and get you."

The other great defensive work was the cutting of the Royal Military Canal from Hythe, below the hills at the back of the Marsh and down to the sea just short of Hastings, a distance of 28 miles. The idea for this came from Major-General John Brown who surveyed the coast for defensive works against Napoleon. It would not only serve as a barrier but would enable troops to be moved quickly by boat from one end of the Marsh to the other. It was estimated to cost £150,000 and the work was entrusted to John Rennie, the engineer who had built both London and Waterloo Bridges. There would be a rampart in front and a military road behind it and it was to be in a zigzag form so that guns, mounted at the bends, could fire down the length of the canal.

Before it could be completed Trafalgar had been fought and Napoleon's invasion called off. Nevertheless it was finished and the final bill came to £234,000.

Some of this money was recovered when the canal was opened for barges and tolls were charged and this proved to be profitable. In 1811 a sum of £770 was collected but against this had to be set the money expended on repairs. During the nineteenth century the canal was earning over £1,000 a year, but traffic slowly dwindled away with the coming of the railways and improved roads.

The Royal Military Canal is now used for pleasure boating only. The Hythe Venetian Fête takes place on it every two years. Some parts are now overgrown with weeds but it is quiet and peaceful, and a stroll along its banks is pleasant in summer. It was defended again in the Second World War and could well have played an important part if Hitler's troops had landed.

A song in praise of the Men of Kent, written at the time of Napoleon's threatened invasion, has the verse:

When royal George commanded
Militia to be raised.

The French would sure have landed
But for such youths as these.
Their oxen stall and cricket ball
They left for martial glory.
The Kentish lads shall win the odds
Your fathers did before you.
Then sing in praise of Men of Kent
All loyal brave and free
Of Briton's race if one surpass
A Man of Kent is he.

Romney Marsh has the well-deserved reputation of being the great smuggling area in the eighteenth and nineteenth centuries. It certainly had a number of advantages for this illegal trade. The French coast is only 30 miles away. It has a long flat shore which, even in these days, is sparsely populated. The area is difficult to patrol for only the local population would know the paths across the marsh. There are many suitable hiding places for smuggled goods and the huge cellars underneath some of the Marsh churches have seen smuggled kegs of brandy in their time.

Smuggling was a very profitable occupation with profits reckoned at 100 per cent. A parliamentary report in 1790 estimated that 50 per cent of the spirits drunk in this country had been smuggled in without the duty being paid on it. France, traditionally a non-tea-drinking country, was importing 6 million pounds of tea every year, most of which was destined for the smuggling trade to England.

Labourers could earn a guinea a night humping the smuggled goods up from the beach and it was generally accepted that they would work on the farms during the summer and work for the smugglers during the winter. In 1735 the Kent farmers were forced to raise the farm labourers' wages to keep them on for the harvest as the men were making more money smuggling.

Smuggling was not regarded by the population as a criminal act, rather as a means of obtaining goods which they otherwise could not have afforded. All classes of the community, land-holders, magistrates and even parsons, were in league with the smugglers. Even when caught and hauled before the bench the smuggler was almost certain to go free as magistrates would not convict. At Deal a band of smugglers rushed into the court, overturned a table on to the constables and freed their comrades. At Dover they broke open the gaol and released a smuggler while the constables looked on helplessly.

Although always prepared to take on the customs men in battle, the smugglers did not look for trouble and preferred to land their goods by stealth. One smuggler had kegs of brandy coated in plaster of Paris so that they looked like lumps of chalk. He then dumped them beneath the white cliffs at Dover where they were collected at leisure by his colleagues. A Folkestone gang had hollow masts on their boats. These were filled with tobacco and unshipped and carried off under the noses of the customs men. Another trick was to have tobacco woven into the ship's ropes.

Visitors to Dymchurch look in vain for evidence of the most famous smuggler of all. Dr Syn's name does not appear on the list of vicars in the church for he was a fictional character. He appears in the books of Russell Thorndike as the leader of the Romney Marsh smugglers who constantly outwitted the authorities. He was a parson by day and smuggler by night. Many people call in at the church at Dymchurch to look for his name on the roll.

Travel across Romney Marsh to the west and in a few minutes we are out of Kent and into Sussex.

This, then, is the end of the journey through this county full of history but there is yet more to be seen than the sites described in these pages. There is the ancient Pilgrims' Way along which Chaucer's pilgrims trudged to Canterbury, "the holy blissful martyr for to seek". There is the house where H. G. Wells lived and wrote *Kipps* and *The History of Mr Polly*. There is a fifteenth-century house which was moved bodily from Sussex into Kent. There is an eleventh-century Norman manor house which is the oldest continuously inhabited house in Britain.

"Kent, sir," said Mr Jingle in *Pickwick Papers*. "Everybody knows Kent – apples, cherries, hops and women." To these he might have added the glorious countryside, rolling woodlands, the white cliffs, medieval villages, cricket – and history.

Few people would agree with Henry Ford who said

"History is bunk", but does everyone realize how much enjoyment can be had by visiting these historic sites? These are not the dead sticks and stones of a past age but the living memorials of the great men and women who lived, worked and fought there. At Dover Castle the old warrior Hubert de Burgh breathed defiance from the battlements. The clatter of armour on the stone pavement of Canterbury Cathedral warned Becket that his end was near. At Chartwell, Churchill walked beside the lake and admired his black swans. It takes very little imagination to see these great historical figures in the settings in which they moved.

Few counties can compare with Kent for the beauty of its countryside. Certainly none can compete in historical interest.

Bibliography

Archaeologia Cantiana, the annual publication of the Kent Archaeological Society

H. F. Abell, *Kent and the Great Civil War* (1901)

M. Burrows, *Cinque Ports* (1895)

H. Braun, *English Abbeys* (1971)

H. Braun, *The English Castle* (1936)

E. Hasted, *History and Topographical Survey of the County of Kent* (1797 – 1801)

W. Jerrold, *Highways and Byways in Kent* (1907)

W. Lambarde, *A Perambulation in Kent* (1576 – 1626)

G. W. Meates, *Lullingstone Roman Villa* (1962)

L. B. Larking, *The Domesday Book of Kent* (1869)

J. Newman, *The Buildings of England: North-East and East Kent* (1969)

J. Newman, *The Buildings of England: West Kent and the Weald* (1969)

A. Perval, *The Faversham Gunpowder Industry* (1967)

C. A. R. Radford, *Dover Castle* (1953)

S. E. Rigold, *Eynsford Castle* (1963)

A. D. Saunders, *Deal and Walmer Castles* (1963)

Victoria County History of Kent

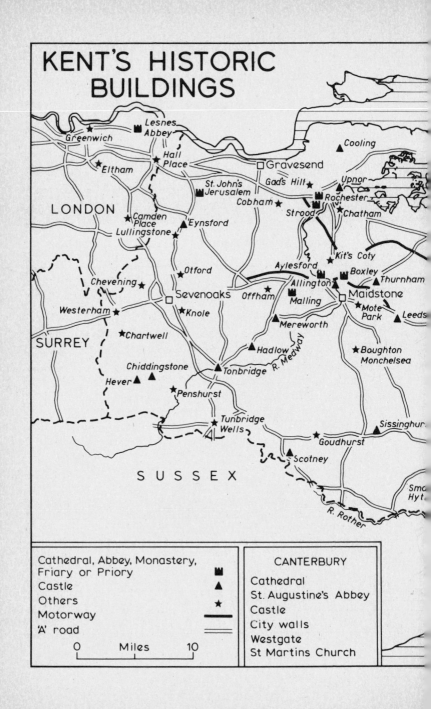

KENT'S HISTORIC BUILDINGS

Greenwich ★

Lesnes 𝔐 Abbey

Cooling ▲

Hall 𝔐 Place

Eltham ★

☐ Gravesend

Upnor ▲

St. John's 𝔐 Jerusalem

Gad's Hill ★

Rochester 𝔐 ▲

LONDON

Cobham ★

Strood 𝔐

Chatham ★

Camden ★ Place

Lullingstone ▲

Eynsford ▲

Kit's Coty ★

Otford ★

Aylesford 𝔐

Boxley ★

Chevening ★

Allington ▲

Thurnham ▲

Sevenoaks ☐

Offham ★

Malling 𝔐

Maidstone ☐

Westerham ★

Knole ★

Mote ★ Park

Leeds ▲

Chartwell ★

Mereworth ▲

Boughton ★ Monchelsea

SURREY

Hadlow ▲

R. Medway

Chiddingstone ▲

Hever ▲

Tonbridge ▲

Penshurst ★

Tunbridge ★ Wells

Sissinghur...

Goudhurst ★

Scotney ★

SUSSEX

Sma... Hyt...

R. Rother

Cathedral, Abbey, Monastery, Friary or Priory	𝔐
Castle	▲
Others	★
Motorway	▬▬▬
'A' road	═══

0   Miles   10

CANTERBURY

Cathedral
St. Augustine's Abbey
Castle
City walls
Westgate
St Martins Church

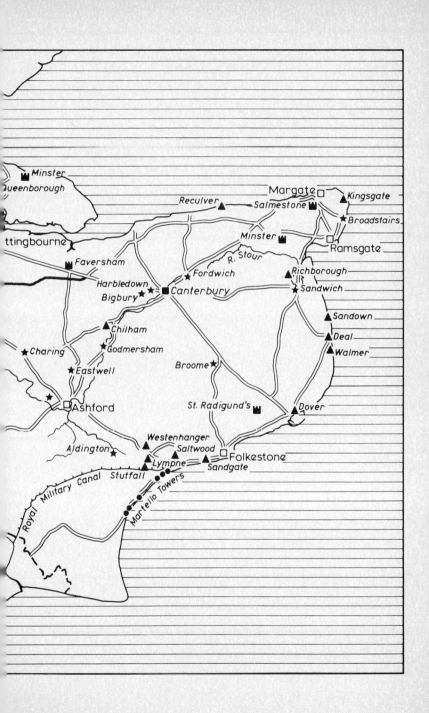

Index